PROCLAMATION:

Aids for Interpreting the
Lessons of the Church Year

SERIES B

David Randolph
and
Jack Kingsbury

FORTRESS PRESS   Philadelphia, Pennsylvania

Library of Congress Catalog Card Number 74-24959

ISBN 0-8006-4076-4

Second printing 1978

7153C78   Printed in the United States of America   1-4076

General Preface

Proclamation: Aids for Interpreting the Lessons of the Church Year is a series of twenty-six books designed to help clergymen carry out their preaching ministry. It offers exegetical interpretations of the lessons for each Sunday and many of the festivals of the church year, plus homiletical ideas and insights.

The basic thrust of the series is ecumenical. In recent years the Episcopal church, the Roman Catholic church, the United Church of Christ, the Christian Church (Disciples of Christ), the United Methodist Church, the Lutheran and Presbyterian churches, and also the Consultation on Church Union have adopted lectionaries that are based on a common three-year system of lessons for the Sundays and festivals of the church year. *Proclamation* grows out of this development, and authors have been chosen from all of these traditions. Some of the contributors are parish pastors; others are teachers, both of biblical interpretation and of homiletics. Ecumenical interchange has been encouraged by putting two persons from different traditions to work on a single volume, one with the primary responsibility for exegesis and the other for homiletical interpretation.

Despite the high percentage of agreement between the traditions, both in the festivals that are celebrated and the lessons that are appointed to be read on a given day, there are still areas of divergence. Frequently the authors of individual volumes have tried to take into account the various textual traditions, but in some cases this has proved to be impossible; in such cases we have felt constrained to limit the material to the Lutheran readings.

The preacher who is looking for "canned sermons" in these books will be disappointed. These books are one step removed from the pulpit: they explain what the lessons are saying and suggest ways of relating this biblical message to the contemporary situation. As such they are springboards for creative thought as well as for faithful proclamation of the word.

The authors of this volume of *Proclamation* are David James Randolph and Jack Dean Kingsbury. Dr. Randolph, the editor-homiletician, is Senior Minister of Christ Church United Methodist in New York City. He was President of the American Academy of Homiletics in 1968-69. Dr. Randolph has taught homiletics at Drew University, Princeton Theological

Seminary, and The Divinity School of Vanderbilt University. He has also served as a denominational executive in the field of worship. Dr. Randolph is the author of *The Renewal of Preaching* (Fortress Press, 1968) and *God's Party* (Abingdon Press, 1975). He is also the editor of the *Ventures in Worship* series (Abingdon Press). Dr. Kingsbury, the exegete, is Associate Professor of New Testament at Union Theological Seminary in Richmond, Va. He is a graduate of Concordia Seminary, St. Louis, Mo. (B.A., B.D.) and the University of Basel (Dr. Theol.). In addition to numerous articles in scholarly journals, Dr. Kingsbury has written two books: *The Parables of Jesus in Matthew 13* (S.P.C.K. and John Knox Press, 1969) and *Matthew: Structure, Christology, Kingdom* (Fortress Press, 1975).

Introduction

The purpose of this volume is to support the preaching ministry by offering exegetical and homiletical interpretations of the lessons for Pentecost Sunday and the nine subsequent Sundays of Series B in the three-year series of lessons of the church year.

The pattern in this volume will be to present the exegetical study in a way which deals both with the uniqueness of each lesson and its relatedness to the other lessons of the day with special attention to the unifying theme, or intentionality, of the texts. This intentionality becomes the *concern* of the sermon, the major meaning to be communicated. This *concern* will then be related to *confirmations* (material which corroborates, ingrains, illustrates) and *concretions* (material which deals with the concrete responsibilities, decisions, actions). Attention will then be paid to possibilities of *construction* by which the message of the text may come to expression in the situation of the hearers.

This pattern is designed for the person who understands preaching to be a creative process. The authors have sought to make important materials available so that from the preacher's own unique angle of vision he may allow the creative spirit to make the truth real to the particular congregation which is to be addressed. Interpretation is one task with many acts. It is the preacher himself who unites the diverse acts into one task of meaningful interpretation. The exegetical movement is basic. Here the spokesman seeks to understand by the best scholarly means available the original intention of the text, i.e., what the text *said*. The homiletical movement extends the exegetical into the present situation of the hearers, i.e., what the text *says*. The preaching event—the actual presentation of the sermon—occurs when the meaning of the biblical text is interpreted into the concrete situation of the hearers in a transforming way.

Jack Dean Kingsbury, the exegete of these lessons, has written of them: "The new three-year lectionary system is so devised that it focuses attention each year on one of the Synoptic Gospels. The Fourth Gospel is used to supply the readings for special feasts and festivals. In recognition of this principle, the discussion of the Scripture readings appointed for each Sunday begins in this book with the Gospel for the day. The strength of this approach is not only that the Gospel reading receives the position of stress, but also that it is followed in each case by a treatment of the OT reading, which as a rule has been chosen precisely because it can be correlated with the Gospel reading. Once the internal affinities between these two texts have been observed, one can move the more easily to a study of the second lesson, which may or may not be related thematically to the other two readings. On the matter of text selection in general, it soon becomes apparent to anyone working with the readings appointed for Pentecost 1 that remarkably good judgment has determined their choice."

Exegetically, the stress falls on the Gospel lesson for theological as well as practical reasons. Homiletically, however, the stress may fall on the second lesson or the OT lesson because that text offers the more compelling vehicle for communication in a specific situation. Whatever lesson may become the preaching text, the sermon should be responsible to the underlying intentionality of OT, Gospel, and Epistle.

Moreover, it must not be assumed that we can simply jump from exegesis to sermon, from what the text said originally to what the text says. We are historical beings. The texts also have a history of interpretation which must be taken into account. Moreover, we are interpreters of the Christian faith and not merely commentators on scattered texts. The question of dogmatics or systematic theology must be dealt with. Through all this we are communicators, sensitive to the people whom we are addressing. Therefore, we look for the material which will confirm the meaning of the text and the concrete ways in which this meaning will come to expression in the lives of the hearers.

These are exceedingly complex matters. Yet, the preacher consciously or unconsciously must deal with them for every sermon. This heightens the challenge of a book like this, for it is not presented as a complete road map to a territory already charted. Rather it is an invitation to an adventure in search of the Word that saves.

To Mrs. Jacqueline Danyo who typed the homiletical portions of this manuscript, the editor expresses thanks.

David James Randolph

Table of Contents

The Day of Pentecost

Lutheran	Roman Catholic	Episcopal	Pres./UCC/Chr.	Methodist/COCU
Ezek. 37:1–14	Acts 2:1–11	Joel 2:28–32	Joel 2:28–32	Joel 2:28–32
Acts 2:1–21	1 Cor. 12:3b–7, 12–13	Rom. 8:14–17, 22–27	Acts 2:1–13	Acts 2:1–21
John 7:37–39a	John 20:19–23	Luke 11:9–13	John 16:5–15	John 16:5–15

EXEGESIS

On the festival of Pentecost, the church celebrates its "founding" by commemorating the outpouring of the Holy Spirit upon the disciples. According to John, Jesus imparted the Holy Spirit to his disciples on the same day on which he arose (20:19–23). According to Luke, the Holy Spirit descended on the disciples on the Jewish feast of Pentecost (Acts 2:1), which was fifty days after Jesus' resurrection. As far as the church calendar is concerned, it is of course the Lucan scheme that has determined the date for the Christian celebration of Pentecost. Nevertheless, the Scripture readings for the day invite us to take a synoptic look at theological emphases drawn from both John and Luke, and Ezekiel as well. In combination, these emphases suggest the unifying thought for the day: Jesus, the author of salvation, is the dispenser of the Spirit (Gospel), who renews God's people (First Lesson) and empowers them to proclaim the word of salvation to persons everywhere (Second Lesson). As dictated by this thought, the mood of Pentecost is one of joyful anticipation: Christian worshipers await once again the descent of the Spirit, who will enable them to respond to God's grace in Christ with a life of witness and service.

Gospel: John 7:37–39a. Chap. 7 is a well-defined unit in John's Gospel. It reaches its culmination in the words of the text, which is embedded in a context of controversy. Jesus' opponents are out to kill him (v. 1). In teaching in the temple (v. 14), Jesus claims for his words and deeds the authority of God (vv. 16–18, 21). Some people hear him and believe (v. 31), but the Pharisees send officers to arrest him (v. 32). With great solemnity Jesus pronounces the words of the text, which create division among the crowd and confound the arresting officers (vv. 43–44).

V. 37 opens with a reference to the "last, great day of the feast." This

Jewish feast, however, is not that of Pentecost (Lev. 23:15–21) but of Tabernacles (7:2; Lev. 23:39–43). To avoid confusing the hearers, therefore, the preacher should perhaps forego explanation of the historical background of these feasts and concentrate instead on the words of Jesus. These words in vv. 37b–38 admit of two quite different ways of punctuation. The first has traditionally been favored by the eastern church and is found in the RSV: "If any one thirst, let him come to me and drink. He who believes in me, as the Scripture has said, 'Out of his heart shall flow rivers of living waters.' " Should the text be read in this manner, then it is the "believer," and not Jesus, from whom the "rivers of living water" flow. The difficulty with this, however, is that elsewhere in his Gospel John does not speak of the believer in specifically these terms.

The second way in which vv. 37b–38 can be punctuated has been advocated historically by the western church and is found in the NEB: "If anyone is thirsty let him come to me; whoever believes in me, let him drink. As Scripture says, 'Streams of living water shall flow out from within him.' " So punctuated, these words now point to Jesus himself as the one from whom the "streams of living water" flow. The reason for preferring this reading is that it enjoys the support of other passages in which John portrays Jesus as the dispenser of "living water" (cf. 4:10, 14; also 19:34). Then, too, we know from v. 39 that the image of "living water" applies to the Spirit; but in John's Gospel, it is exclusively Jesus or the Father who gives the Spirit (20:22; 15:26; 16:7–15).

V. 39 is a parenthetical remark John makes in order to put the entire passage into proper theological perspective. "Water" was well known to the Jews as a symbol for spirit and pointed to the coming age of salvation (cf. Isa. 12:3). In that John depicts Jesus as the one from whom the waters of salvation, or the Holy Spirit, flow, so he is affirming that in the person of Jesus salvation is a present reality. In the Fourth Gospel, the work of the Spirit is to "bear witness" to Jesus (14:26; 15:26; 16:12–15). By so doing, the Spirit mediates salvation, or "life," to those who "believe" in Jesus, that is to say, to those who confess him to be the "Christ, the Son of God" (20:31). The new life which is in Jesus and is mediated by the Spirit to the church—this is the message this Gospel text proclaims on the occasion of Pentecost.

First Lesson: Ezek. 37:1–14. Ezekiel discharged his prophetic ministry over a period of more than twenty years (593–571 B.C.) as an exile in Babylon (1:1, 3; 33:21; 40:1). The destruction of Jerusalem and of the temple in 586 B.C. caused him and his fellow Israelites no little consternation. Whereas in the forepart of his book Ezekiel inveighs against the sins of his people (chaps. 2–24) and pronounces oracles of doom against the surrounding nations (chaps. 25–32), in the latter part of his book he foretells the future restoration of both Israel and the temple (chaps. 33–48). Our text is situated in the latter section.

In the vision of the valley of dry bones, made famous by the celebrated Negro spiritual, Ezekiel describes himself as caught up by God and transported to a wide plain that was strewn with the bones of countless men long dead (vv. 1–2). Asked by God whether these bones would ever live again, Ezekiel has no answer (v. 4). But God commands him to prophesy breath and life for these bones (vv. 4–6). Ezekiel obeys, and to his astonishment the bones order themselves once again as bodies (vv. 7–8). By means of a second prophecy these bodies receive breath, or life, and the "exceedingly great host" then takes to its feet (vv. 9–10).

In vv. 11–14, Ezekiel explains his vision. The dry bones represent the house of Israel (v. 11). Cut off from the temple and without hope, these exiles are as dead and buried (vv. 11–12). In the power of his Spirit, however, God opens their graves and restores them to life. What Ezekiel predicts, therefore, is that God will give proof of his Lordship by returning Israel to her land and reconstituting her as a nation (vv. 13–14).

The theme of this text is not that of resurrection per se. Rather, it proclaims faith (v. 3) in the power, or Spirit, of God to imbue a people, despite utterly hopeless circumstances, with that life that only God can give (vv. 13–14). For Christians, the new people of God, such life is theirs by virtue of God's grace in Jesus and is the gift of the Holy Spirit in word and sacrament.

Second Lesson: Acts 2:1–21. The setting for the extraordinary events surrounding the day of Pentecost is Jerusalem (Acts 1:4). For Luke, Jerusalem is not merely a geographical location but is also of theological significance: it is the place of temptation (Luke 4:9–13) and of death (Luke 9:31; 13:33; 18:31–32). Thus, the way of Jesus is towards Jerusalem, where he suffers, dies, and rises (Luke 9:51; 18:31–32). By contrast, the way of the church is from Jerusalem towards Rome (Acts 1:8), occasioned to no small degree by the same manner of rejection Jesus encountered (Acts 4–9).

The text divides itself into three parts: it tells of the outpouring of the Holy Spirit upon the disciples (vv. 1–4), of the reaction to their preaching by the great crowd of Jews and proselytes (vv. 5–13), and of the first half of Peter's speech to the crowd (vv. 14–21).

Gathered together in a house, the disciples are filled with the Holy Spirit (vv. 1–4). The sudden sound from heaven of the rush of a mighty wind (v. 2) portends the approach of the Spirit (v. 4). The "tongues as of fire" (v. 3) point at once to the gift the disciples receive to "speak in other tongues" (v. 4) and the fact that the word they will proclaim will effect division, or judgment, among people (cf. Luke 12:49–53). The phenomenon itself of "speaking in tongues" seems to refer here to the ability to discourse in other recognizable languages (vv. 6, 8, 11).

At the speaking of the disciples in other languages, a huge crowd of Jews and proselytes from many nations gathers and asks as to the significance of this (vv. 5–12). The names of the lands and regions cited can be correlated with the signs of the zodiac, the inference being that Luke's geographical catalogue constitutes a representative list of all the nations of the world. Consequently, one purpose of the text is to show that the word of the "mighty works of God" (v. 11), which the disciples proclaim in many languages on Pentecost, is able to dispel the confusion of tongues that long ago resulted from humankind's presumptuous effort to find its unity in its own strength, in the construction of the tower of Babel (Gen. 11:1–9).

In response to the taunt that the disciples are perhaps drunk (v. 13), Peter addresses the crowd and interprets what is taking place as the outpouring of the Holy Spirit in fulfillment of the prophecy of Joel (vv. 14–21). According to Peter's speech, a new time has dawned (vv. 17, 20), for Jesus, crucified, raised, and exalted to the right hand of God, has now poured out the Holy Spirit upon his disciples (vv. 22–33). Empowered by the Spirit, the disciples bear witness in these last days to God's mighty acts in Jesus (Acts 1:8), and the word they proclaim is one of salvation: it summons all people, Jew and Gentile, to call upon the name of the Lord and be saved (v. 21).

Accordingly, the major thought of the text is that empowered and therefore guided by the Holy Spirit, the disciples of Jesus attest to God's mighty acts in him and so proclaim the word of salvation which is meant for all people.

HOMILETICAL INTERPRETATION

1. CONCERN

Jesus imparts the Spirit who renews God's people and empowers them to proclaim the word of salvation with joyful anticipation to persons everywhere.

2. CONFIRMATIONS AND CONCRETIONS

The valley full of bones is one of the most contemporary of ancient images. It represents life outracing its limits, the abandonment of hope, ultimate desolation.

Ezekiel's vision is our reality. As real as My Lai, Dachau, Hiroshima. As real as burned out buildings in Dresden and the South Bronx. As real as the weariness which leads us to say at times, "I am bone tired."

The Mexican artist, Jose Guadalupe Posada, developed a large corpus of work showing persons engaged in a wide range of activities but depicted as skeletons. In one drawing he depicted a soldier riding through a valley of bones full of skulls.[1] Picasso's work "Guernica" expresses in one master painting the skeletal consequences of war. Terrible as that state is, however, it is overcome early in Ezekiel's vision: the prophet speaks and the bones come together. Sinews cover the bones; next skin covers the flesh.

Then comes the most terrifying aspect: bodies to all appearances human but without the breath of life. This is the essence of tragedy— not that we die but that we do not live. The flesh without spirit, not the dry bones, is the most haunting aspect of the vision. It is the zombie, the living dead, who is even a more frightening representation of our time than the skeleton.

These are the bodies T. S. Eliot described in "The Waste Land." Movement I, "The Burial of the Dead," refers to interment not in the cemetery but in the modern city. We see a crowd of people flowing across the London Bridge, sighing, each with his eyes fixed before his feet. The poet had not thought that "death had undone so many."[2]

The Day of the Locust by Nathanael West shifts the scene to Hollywood.[3] There a commercial artist, Tod Hackett, works on a master painting to be called "The Burning of Los Angeles." Before the painting can be completed, however, Hackett is crushed in a mob which riots while awaiting the arrival of movie stars at a premiere. The novel ends with Hackett's scream blending with the sound of the police siren, even as his fantasy blends with the reality of his painting.

This novel, and the film of it directed by John Schlesinger, is about the people who slave at dull jobs until they save enough to go to California— the land of dreams. Once there they discover that sunshine and oranges

1. See Justino Fernandes, *A Guide to Mexican Art* (Chicago and London: University of Chicago Press, 1969), especially p. 154.

2. T. S. Eliot, *Collected Poems 1909–1962* (New York: Harcourt, Brace & World: 1930–1963). "The Waste Land," with notes, is found on pp. 51–76. "The Hollow Men," pp. 79–82, carries on the theme. "Ash Wednesday," pp. 83–95, employs the "dry bones" imagery from Ezekiel in Movement II.

3. Nathanael West, *The Day of the Locust*, with an introduction by Richard B. Gehman (New York: Bantam Book, 1959).

are not enough. One wave of the Pacific looks just like the one which came before. The American continent and the Dream end at the Pacific. These people haven't the personal resources to improve their situation and long for excitement and violence to pull their senses tight. They feel cheated and betrayed.

The novel is not about the big stars and producers of the film world, but the *pretenders* who seek the meaning of their lives by assuming the poses of celebrities. West's vision cuts to the bone of our modern malaise: our capacity to imitate has outrun our capacity to create. We have traded the humble but holy reality of our lives for the spectacular illusion.

The valley of dry bones cuts through the Hollywood Hills across the continent, and throughout the world. It is an inescapable region in the landscape of our time.

The word of the Lord which brought flesh to the bones in Ezekiel's vision was summoned again and this time brought the Spirit which gives life to the flesh. Jesus Christ was that word incarnate. Jesus is to spiritual dryness what a spring of water is to thirst. The Christian faith knows of no other source from which "the streams of living water flow." There is no way out of the valley full of bones except by way of the mountain full of life, Calvary. Only the Day of the Lord is more potent than the Day of the Locust.

Nathanael West also had a glimpse of this possibility which he shared in *Miss Lonelyhearts*, the story of a writer of an advice-to-the-lovelorn column. "Miss Lonelyhearts," actually a man, reads through the correspondence which floods him with the lamentations of persons suffering from kidney pain, from unwanted pregnancy, from being born without a nose, from those assaulted by others and by their own endless fears. He stops reading. He knows that Christ is the answer to these cries, but feels that he had better stay away from "the Christ business."

"Miss Lonelyhearts" becomes sick and his view of religion is part of this sickness. Yet, as a boy in his father's church, he had discovered that when he shouted the name of Christ something powerful stirred within him. Then West offers what may be the explanation of the sickness of "Miss Lonelyhearts": "He had played with this (Christ) thing but had never allowed it to come alive."[4]

We stay in the valley full of bones as long as we "play" with Christ without really letting him come alive.

The Day of Pentecost marks the advent of hope as the valley of bones marks the advent of despair. It might be said that until that day the

4. Nathanael West, *Miss Lonelyhearts*, with an introduction by Stanley Edgar Hyman (New York: Avon Books, 1955–1964), p. 42.

early church had been "playing" with Christ. Playing, not altogether frivolously, but in the sense that they had not allowed the fullness of his power to occupy them. Then on the Day of Pentecost, Christ really came alive. The something for which they had longed, happened.

The imagery of the event is incandescent. It glows with tongues of fire and the bewilderment of other languages. People stagger like drunken men. But when Peter speaks and the air clears that which is testified to is nothing other than the mighty works of God.

That mighty work goes on in the church wherever the dreams of the old and the visions of the young refuse to "play" with Christ but allow the risen Christ to come alive. For this mighty work is the work of salvation: "Whoever calls on the name of the Lord shall be saved."

Now what concrete response can be given to such a mighty event? Here we are at the very heart of man's response to the gospel. Man's predicament without God is so desperate and man's possibilities with God are so enormous that any response seems incidental. Does one fall to his knees in prayer? Does one rise to his feet in service? Does one do both? In what sequence?

Such questions are secondary. They come at a distance from the event and may be a form of "playing" with Christ. Anyone who places himself within the event of Pentecost knows the answer of faith: Repent and be baptized, receive the Holy Spirit.

Repentance is the radical turning of the whole self from itself to orientation to God. To be baptized is to enter into the life of the church. To receive the Holy Spirit is to allow the Spirit to shape our lives in obedient witness and service. It may mean selling what we don't need, distributing our goods to the needy, sharing a common life with others, worshiping daily and breaking bread in homes—as it did to the early Christian community described in Acts 2:37–47.

In our time it will certainly mean the distribution of the waters of grace into the valley of dry bones where life is dehumanized and destroyed. This will take many concrete acts of witness and service in a lifetime of commitment. But unless these acts are to evaporate and lead back to the valley of dry bones, they must proceed from that repentance which is the total turning of self to God.

3. CONSTRUCTION

The concern of these texts unfolds logically and poetically from OT lesson, to Gospel, to Second Lesson. If the essay form is used, each text may supply a point. For example:

1. Life without faith is desperate.

2. Life with Christ overcomes despair.
3. Life with Christ finds empowerment through the Spirit in the church for mission in the world.

A more poetic development would cluster symbols around three master images. For example:

1. The Day of the Locust.
2. The Day of the Lord.
3. The Day of Pentecost.

In either case the sermon, theologically and structurely, finds its center in the Gospel.

The Holy Trinity,
The First Sunday after Pentecost

Lutheran	*Roman Catholic*	*Episcopal*	*Pres./UCC/Chr.*	*Methodist/COCU*
Deut. 6:4–9	Deut. 4:32–34, 39–40	Exod. 3:1–6	Isa. 6:1–8	Deut. 4:32–34, 39–40
2 Cor. 13:11–14	Rom. 8:14–17	Acts 2:32–39	Rom. 8:12–17	Rom. 8:12–17
John 3:1–17	Matt. 28:16–20	John 3:1–16	John 3:1–8	Matt. 28:16–20

EXEGESIS

Gospel: John 3:1–17. As the Gospel reading for Trinity Sunday, this text has been appointed because it makes direct reference to God the Father, to his Son Jesus, and to the Holy Spirit. Indeed, one way of outlining the text serves to highlight each of the three: vv. 3–8 pertain above all to the Spirit, vv. 11–15 to the Son of man, and vv. 16–17 to God.

Vv. 1–8 focus on the theme of "begetting from above." John reports that Nicodemus, who is a Pharisee, a member of the Sanhedrin, and a teacher, comes to Jesus by night to converse with him (vv. 1–2, 10). He is the spokesman, as it were, of those Jews who had seen the signs Jesus did during the feast of the Passover and had consequently begun to believe in him (v. 2; 2:23). Nicodemus initiates the dialogue by telling Jesus that he considers him to be a teacher approved by God (v. 2). To this Jesus solemnly replies that unless a person is begotten from above, he is unable to experience the gracious rule of God (v. 3).

Nicodemus misconstrues Jesus' words. He understands "begotten from above" as "being born again," and therefore asks Jesus how it is possible for a man to enter his mother's womb a second time and be born once more (v. 4). Jesus does not give specific answer to this query, but instead speaks of the working of the "Spirit." Nicodemus, however, still does not understand him, for he takes the word "Spirit" to mean "wind." More particularly, Jesus tells Nicodemus that a person, simply as he is by nature, that is to say, simply as one born into the world by reason of his father's begetting him, is unable to enter into the sphere of God's rule; to enter this sphere, what is necessary is that one be begotten "from above," that is to say, regenerated by the power of God's Spirit (vv. 5–7). Moreover, such regeneration by the Spirit is something that is beyond human comprehension and accomplishment; it can only be effected by the Spirit himself: even as the "wind blows where it wills, and you hear the sound of it, but you do not know whence it comes or whither it goes," so the "Spirit breathes where he wills, and you hear his voice, but you do not know whence he comes or whither he goes" (v. 8).

In response to Jesus' words, Nicodemus puts one more question to him, thereby giving evidence of his continued ignorance as to what Jesus is talking about (v. 9). In reply, Jesus chides Nicodemus (vv. 10–11), but does tell him how regeneration by the Spirit takes place. It takes place, says Jesus, through faith in the Son of Man, whom God has decreed should be "lifted up" on the cross. Regenerated by the Spirit through faith in the Son of man, a person receives the gift of "eternal life" (vv. 14–15).

In conclusion of his dialogue with Nicodemus, Jesus broadens the scope of the discussion by pointing to God as the ultimate source of salvation (v. 16). His great love for humankind is what has impelled him to send his Son into the world and to the cross (v. 16). Through faith in the Son, people need not perish but can receive the gift of eternal life mediated by the Spirit, and so be saved (vv. 16–17).

In sum, the main point of this text is that one receives salvation, or eternal life, as the gift of the Spirit through faith in the Son, whose coming into the world and death on the cross are God's absolute demonstration of his great love for humankind.

First Lesson: Deut. 6:4–9. In chap. 5, the Deuteronomist depicts Moses as reminding Israel of the covenant God has made with her and of its statutes and ordinances. Chap. 6, in which we find the text, has to do with the meaning of the so-called First Commandment (v. 1).

The text is known in Jewish tradition as the "Shema," after the Hebrew word with which v. 4 begins and which means "hear." The Shema captures in a word the faith of Israel, and is Judaism's highest confession. On the basis of the words of v. 7, ". . . when you lie down, and when you rise," rabbinic law early stipulated that the faithful Jew should recite the Shema both morning and evening.

Vv. 4–5 are essentially a restatement in positive form of the First Commandment of the Decalogue (cf. 5:7–10). This is termed *"the* commandment" in v. 1, and was known as such also by Jesus (Mark 12:28–30; Matt. 22:36–38). The point of v. 4 is that there are not many gods or forces in the universe but one Lord, who is unique and sovereign (cf. 4:39). The point of v. 5 is that one is to love the one, sovereign God utterly and completely.

By postexilic times, if not earlier, v. 8 was taken literally and thus gave rise to the custom of wearing phylacteries. Phylacteries are small leather receptacles in cubical form which every male Jew above thirteen years of age was required to tie on himself, one on the left arm and one on the forehead, during morning prayer. Whereas the phylactery for the arm had one compartment, that for the forehead had four. Each compartment contained a piece of parchment on which was written one (or, in the case of the arm phylactery, all four) of the OT passages that were regarded as giving sanction to the practice (Exod. 13:1–10, 11–16; Deut. 6:4–9; 11:13–21).

On Trinity Sunday, the reading of the Shema is most appropriate. It reminds Christians that though they worship three persons, God is nevertheless in essence one.

Second Lesson: 2 Cor. 13:11–14. The text culminates in v. 14 with what has become a familiar Christian benediction. The great creeds of the church are, from one standpoint, later theological elaborations of passages such as this (cf. Matt. 28:19).

V. 11 reflects the fact that the Corinthian congregation had been wracked by factionalism and dissension. False Jewish-Christians from Palestine with Gnostic-pneumatic tendencies had invaded the congregation with a theology of glory, deprecating Paul's theology of the cross. Combined with this was a fierce attack on the very person and apostleship of Paul, against which the latter vigorously defended himself (2:14–7:4). In v. 11, then, Paul bids the congregation farewell and urges the members to pull themselves together, to encourage one another, and to let harmony and peace prevail. If they do so, Paul assures them that God will himself bless them by showering his own love and peace upon them.

In v. 12, mention is made of "greeting one another with a holy kiss." It appears that at the very least this was a liturgical gesture that had its place in the celebration of the Lord's Supper and gave demonstration of the fellowship that united all Christians as members of God's end-time people in Christ (cf. Rom. 16:16; 1 Cor. 16:20; 1 Thess. 5:26).

The meaning of the benediction in v. 14 is that the grace which Jesus Christ, who is now Lord of the church, has manifested towards human-kind in the cross (2 Cor. 8:9) flows from the love of God, which love also enables Christians to participate in the life of the Spirit (cf. Gal. 6:18; Phil. 4:23). This thought tallies well with the Gospel for Trinity Sunday.

HOMILETICAL INTERPRETATION

1. CONCERN

The one God reveals himself in love as Father, Son, and Holy Spirit.

2. CONFIRMATIONS AND CONCRETIONS

The homiletical emphasis for this Trinity Sunday clearly falls with the Gospel lesson dealing, as it does, with the Trinity. The Trinity is approached existentially, that is, through the concrete situations of the existence of Nicodemus. The sermon has rich resources, for Nicodemus is one of the most intriguing persons recorded in the Scriptures.

Nicodemus was a ruler of the Jews. He was a teacher of Israel. He was a big man in Jerusalem. Nicodemus is a very "modern" type of man. Picture him as he would, and probably does, appear in your city or town.

Nicodemus has it made. And yet he is not quite sure why he wakes in the night. Nor is he sure why he wakes in the morning. The point of his life has grown dull. Perhaps he has lost it altogether. We can imagine him on a restless night going to Jesus, the visiting preacher, with the hope that perhaps this new figure on the religious horizon will be able to offer what he is looking for, even though he is not sure what that is.

When Nicodemus finds Jesus he begins with a complimentary approach. Jesus must have looked not so much at Nicodemus as through him. In effect he says, "Oh Nicodemus, come off it. Why are you giving me this Madison Avenue stuff? Are you wanting to fit me into a comfortable niche in your comfortable life? Are you hoping somehow that religion is going to be just another trophy you can put on your shelf? Nicodemus, face it. I am involved in a kingdom of the Spirit. You are not going to be able to fit this kingdom into your life, your life is going to have to fit into this kingdom. You must be born again."

Today we don't find Jesus' words any more comfortable than Nicodemus did. We, too, would like the world of the Spirit to be another thing in our well-ordered lives. We would like the kingdom of God to be one of the many places we could visit on some future itinerary.

But there is something in the nature of spiritual reality which will not let us rest with that. No matter how materialistic we may be, no matter how absorbed we may be in our quest for success, we sense somehow another possibility. We may sense it with the sophistication of an Edward Arlington Robinson who saw a dark night all around him in his poem entitled "Credo." Yet even Robinson felt "the coming glory of the Light." Less sophisticated were the dance-hall girls pictured in the Broadway show and film, "Sweet Charity." Night after night they danced with any man who had the money to buy their time. Always there was the hope that someone would come in and dance them into a new life. They sang, "There's got to be something better than this."

No matter how much we get caught up in the material realm there is a wind that blows through our lives. We can't keep it out. This is the wind of the Spirit. The Spirit does not occupy some other world far away. The Spirit occupies a plane which cuts right through all that we do and all that we are. The Spirit isn't located somewhere else but right in the midst of the world where we live and work. To be born of the Spirit is to share that plane and to give it primacy.

Nicodemus' response to Jesus was to attempt to put him down. "Born again . . . Am I to enter a second time into my mother's womb?" Jesus unmasked that evasiveness by insisting that Nicodemus deal with the concrete reality of that very moment. What it came down to was whether or not Nicodemus would accept Jesus as the door by which he was to enter the world of the Spirit.

This is what the NT frankly admits is the scandal of Christianity. For what Christianity is about is not some fairytale in a never, never land. Christianity has to do with the concrete reality of our everyday life. It has to do with whether we are going to find in this man, Jesus, our Lord and Savior. The Christian sees in this Jesus of Nazareth the Son of man and the Son of God. It is a staggering claim which Jesus makes about himself. No wonder that the character in Nathanael West's novel wants to "play" with Christ rather than to deal with him.

We today find it no less scandalous than Nicodemus. Jesus says to us, as he said to him, that we have to choose. We did not choose to be born, but we must choose to be re-born, as Hermann Hesse reminded us. We must choose the name by which we are to be born into the Spirit. And for the Christian that name is Jesus Christ.

We owe an enormous debt to the religions of the world. Personally, I find myself in awe of the truths which come from Judaism, Buddhism, Hinduism, and Islam. I have learned much from them. The world of the

Spirit is infinite and its winds blow from many directions. Christians are those who enter the world of the Spirit through the door of Jesus Christ. Jesus continues with Nicodemus by pointing out that once the name is named, once we open the door to Jesus Christ in the concrete situations of our life, then it is as if a whole universe of energy rushes through that door. Jesus' reference is to a life which is eternal, to a world that is cosmic in its dimensions.

God is the cosmic reality, present in and through Jesus of Nazareth. It is incredible to our normal way of experiencing things. But in the moment when we are able to sense God in this man Jesus, then the whole universe rises up in support. "For God so loved the world that he gave his only begotten Son, that whosoever believeth in him should not perish, but have everlasting life."

We do not know how the encounter between Jesus and Nicodemus ended that night but there are two other references to Nicodemus in the NT: John 7:50 depicts him in his role as a leader of the Jews pleading that a fair chance be given to Jesus; and John 19:39 depicts Nicodemus caring for the body of Jesus which places him very near the crucifixion. We do not know the details of where and when, but at some point this ruler, this man, came to know that "God so loved . . . Nicodemus."

This entire discussion has been about the Trinity. The God of the Christian revelation is the God who meets us as Spirit, as Son, and as Father. This understanding, drawn from the Gospel lesson, is enriched by reference to the OT lesson which emphasizes the oneness of God and the Epistle which stresses his love.

J. S. Whale in his book *Christian Doctrine* sums up the discussion of the Trinity in a way which also sums up these three lessons for the day: "The transcendent God of Israel, who had revealed himself in Christ as the God of infinite grace, was now and always the life-giving Spirit of his Church. . . . The Bible speaks of one God, and of one God only. It speaks of him in three distinct ways which are normative for Christian thinking."[1]

We have been considering the Trinity in its existential meaning rather than in its philosophical presuppositions. In this existential, practical meaning the doctrine of the Trinity teaches us that the God who met Nicodemus in Jesus Christ is the God who meets us here and now.

In relation to the lesson and sermon of last Sunday, this sermon should stress that the Spirit of Pentecost must be "tested" against the Spirit of the God of the Trinity. And in relationship to our lives, this doctrine assures

1. J. S. Whale, *Christian Doctrine* (New York: MacMillan and Cambridge, England: At the University Press, 1941), p. 114.

us that the rebirth which is so desperately needed in our day is no harder for us than it was for Nicodemus. Nor is it easier. Many know that rebirth must come. The Christian knows that it can come through Jesus Christ.

3. CONSTRUCTION

The structure which emerges from the Gospel lesson builds on three distinct supports:

    1. God as Spirit.
    2. God as Son.
    3. God as Father.

The contemporaneity of the passage can be shown by use of the narrative/application method. That is, identifying the major element in each passage of the text then showing its application to contemporary life. The OT lesson and the Epistle relate most directly to the third point. The summary should include both a statement on the Trinity in its existential expression and exposition of how that relates to our life of today, building on confirmations such as those suggested above.

The Second Sunday after Pentecost

Lutheran	*Roman Catholic*	*Episcopal*	*Pres./UCC/Chr.*	*Methodist/COCU*
Deut. 5:12–15	Deut. 5:12–15	Deut. 5:6–21	Deut. 5:12–15	Deut. 5:12–15
2 Cor. 4:5–11	2 Cor. 4:6–11	2 Cor. 4:7–11	2 Cor. 4:6–11	2 Cor. 4:7–11
Mark 2:23–28	Mark 2:23–28	Mark 2:23–28	Mark 2:23–3:6	Mark 2:23–3:6

EXEGESIS

Gospel: Mark 2:23–28. From the second through the ninth Sunday after Pentecost, the Gospel for the day is taken from the first half of Mark.

The story of plucking grain on the sabbath is situated in the first major section of the Gospel (1:14–3:6), which treats the opening phase of Jesus' public ministry in Galilee (1:14–15). The emphasis in this section is on, respectively, the call of the disciples (1:14–20), the miracles Jesus performs (cf. 2:1–12), and his debates with the leaders of the Jews (cf. 2:1–3:6). The section closes on the ominous note that the Pharisees and Herodians go out and hold counsel on how to destroy him (3:6).

The text clearly has the form of a debate: the setting is established (v. 23); the Pharisees lodge a charge against the disciples (v. 24); and

Jesus refutes the charge with his authoritative word (vv. 25–28). Since the reply of Jesus falls into two parts (cf. "And he said to them," v. 27), it is in the latter part, which occupies the position of stress, that we can expect to find the climax of the narrative.

Mark writes that the Pharisees, in a question to Jesus, accuse the disciples of breaking the law because they pluck grain on the sabbath (vv. 23–24). Technically, since the act of gleaning itself is not, according to Deut. 23:24–25, a violation of the law, it would seem that we are to think of Exod. 34:21, a statute that prohibits reaping on the sabbath, as furnishing the grounds for the accusation. However this may be, Jesus responds to the Pharisees with a (double) counter-question, a literary device that is characteristic of rabbinical arguments (cf. Mark 12:10, 26).

To trace the logic of vv. 25–28, the Markan Jesus refutes the charge against the disciples in three steps. The thing to observe is that each step is of greater weight than the preceding one, so that it is in the final one that the answer of Jesus culminates. In vv. 25–26, the purpose for which Jesus recalls the OT story that tells how David and his men, hungry and in need, entered the house of God and ate the holy bread of the Presence (cf. 1 Sam. 21:1–6) is to remind the Pharisees that it has always been permissible, under exceptional circumstances of human need, to set aside the statutes that regulate the sabbath. This illustration alone is tantamount to a rebuttal of the Pharisees' charge against the disciples.

But Mark appends to this two further assertions of Jesus. The first (v. 27) bases the legitimacy of setting aside the sabbath law on the principle of "creational priority": in the order of creation, even as God's making man (Gen. 1:26–31) preceded his institution of the sabbath rest (Gen. 2:1–3), so "the sabbath was made for man, not man for the sabbath." The second assertion (v. 28), which is climactic, bases the legitimacy of the disciples' behavior on the authority of Jesus himself: if v. 27 is true, then Jesus Son of man, who wields the very authority of God, is in the last analysis the one who determines what is permissible on the sabbath.

In sum, the central thought of this text is that it is the will of Jesus, the authoritative Son of man, that compassion and love, not the blind observance of regulations, are to be the hallmark of the Christian life.

First Lesson: Deut. 5:12–15. More than anything else, Deuteronomy concerns itself with the revelation of God's will and with all that this implies. Consequently, the section 4:44–6:3, which depicts Moses as presenting to Israel the Decalogue (5:6–21; cf. Exod. 20:2–17), is central to it. Depending upon how one counts, we may regard the text as the Third Commandment.

The Decalogue begins with a fixed formula by means of which God is portrayed as introducing himself to Israel (5:6). The idea is that with these words the divine "I" is thought to approach Israel and to address her as his own possession. Theologically, this is of great importance for understanding the Decalogue, for it means that God speaks to Israel as one who, in bringing her out of bondage, has already demonstrated his saving will towards her. Accordingly, in that Israel adheres to the Decalogue, she is not saving herself by works, but is responding to the grace God has shown her.

The OT gives two reasons why God should enjoin observance of the sabbath. In Exod. 20:8–11, such observance is explained in terms of creation: God rested on the seventh day from his work and therefore so should humans. By contrast, in Deuteronomy we learn that the purpose of the sabbath is both to provide rest for man and beast (vv. 13–14) and to establish an occasion on which Israel might ponder her deliverance from Egypt (v. 15).

The Gospel text, we saw, places love above casuistry. But Christians are not antinomian per se (cf. Matt. 5:17–20). The text, then, complements the Gospel reading well, for it reminds the church that in response to God's grace in Christ, the Christian, too, does the will of God as expressed in the Decalogue.

Second Lesson: 2 Cor. 4:5–11. The text is a part of the larger section 2:14–7:4 in which Paul speaks of the ministry that has been entrusted to him and explains its purpose. In the text itself, Paul sketches in one sentence the content of his ministry and of his gospel, and then tells of the impact it has upon his life. Although he writes in the first person plural ("we"), Paul's statements are primarily reflective of his own situation.

In v. 5 Paul succinctly describes his ministry and summarizes his gospel. Unlike his Jewish-Christian, Gnostic-pneumatic opponents at Corinth, Paul asserts that he does not preach, or exercise his ministry, so as to secure status for himself (cf. 3:1; 5:12), but so as to proclaim Christ Jesus as Lord and to serve (i.e., to assume pastoral responsibility for) the Corinthian Christians. As a capsule-summary of his gospel, the meaning of the words "Christ Jesus as Lord" is that Jesus of Nazareth, the Messiah who was crucified, has been exalted by God through resurrection to the right hand of power, as a result of which he is presently Lord of all (cf. Rom. 10:9; 1 Cor. 1:18; 2:2; 12:3; 15:3–4). The relationship for Paul between gospel and ministry is that to accept the gospel, that is, to acknowledge Christ Jesus as Lord, is both to be saved (Rom. 10:9) and to become his slave (Rom. 1:1; Phil. 1:1). But to become the slave of Christ is likewise to become the slave ("pastor") of those who are his (e.g., the Corinthians).

Paul traces the origin of his ministry to God himself (v. 6). The very God who in the beginning created light (Gen. 1:3) is the one who has enlightened him. In the encounter with Christ on the road to Damascus, God made the glory of his saving ways known to Paul. Through his ministry, Paul now shares this knowledge with others.

Thus, it is "earthenware vessels," frail human beings such as Paul, to whom the "treasure" of the gospel has been entrusted (v. 7a). In this way, the source of the extraordinary power of the gospel for salvation will always reveal itself to be God and not Paul (v. 7b). Indeed, no matter what the experience that threatens to crush Paul, God's power sustains him (vv. 8–9). And although his life is such that he is gradually being killed for the sake of Christ, through him the resurrected Christ makes manifest the new life that is his (vv. 10–11).

Whereas the First Lesson and the Gospel point out, respectively, that obedience towards God and love towards others are hallmarks of the Christian life, this text brings the two thoughts together: to know Christ Jesus as Lord is to serve him by serving one's fellows.

HOMILETICAL INTERPRETATION

1. Concern

God has faced us in Jesus Christ and therefore we can face him and our world with confidence and joy.

2. Confirmations and Concretions

Nobody likes to be left in the dark. At the physical level it is frightening and we try to avoid it with costly lighting systems.

Nobody likes to be left in the dark figuratively. We want to be in the know, not in the dark. To be in a situation where we don't know what is going on is threatening. And yet the truth of the matter is that for a great deal of our lives, we *are* in the dark.

Who of us, for example, thinking about his or her past feels completely in the know about their own life? Can we speak with certainty about who we are? About the forces that have made us? About how we got here? When we look back on our own lives in many ways we are in the dark.

Who of us in thinking about his or her future can speak with assurance? Who can predict accurately our economy? Our relations to our friends? Our employment? When we think about our future much of it is in the dark.

The great power of the Christian faith is that while we may be in the dark about many things in terms of the ultimate issues of human existence, there is light. The God who created heaven and earth and who commanded the light to shine out of darkness, has not left us in the dark. "We have seen the light of the glory of God in the face of Jesus Christ." We may never be able to get quite straight all the details of our past nor our future, but there is no doubt that God's love is eternal and that this love shines from the face of Jesus Christ. No matter how dark our situation may be, the splendor and the radiance of God shines forth in the face of Jesus Christ.

God could have made all kinds of spectacular displays for his glory. Yet he chose to make his ultimate revelation in a human face—a face like yours and like mine. The ordinariness of the human face is in itself a mark of the uniqueness of the Christian revelation. So when we ask who and where is God? the answer is the face of Jesus Christ, a face like yours, a face like mine.

Most of us at some point in our life have seen glory in a face. A mother, a father, a teacher, a preacher, a truck driver, a shop keeper has given us a glimpse of the glory of God. I imagine that few of us would be Christians if there were not a face like that in our lives. But in someone, somewhere, we saw a face in which there was such peace, joy, and togetherness rooted in Christ that had we not been a Christian we would have wanted to become one because of the glory in that face.

Because of that we turn toward God with confidence. Because Jesus has shown us his face we do not cringe before some overpowering cosmic bully, we do not bow in obeisance before the raw forces of nature. Rather ultimate reality has turned toward us and shown us a face to which we can relate with trust and love.

Because God has turned his face toward us, we can turn our face toward the world. We can face life with its problems and perplexities. We can face the problems of the world creatively and redemptively. The OT lesson today draws our attention to the importance of moral law. We are to observe the sabbath day. The Gospel lesson, however, describes a situation in which Jesus found himself in conflict with the law as the Pharisees understood it. The Pharisees held that Jesus was breaking the law when he plucked grain and ate it on the sabbath.

Yet, we may argue that Jesus was keeping the law in its central meaning when he placed dealing with hunger above keeping the letter of the law. In our time hunger has reached global proportions. It is common knowledge that the United States with a relatively small portion of the world's population possesses and uses a disproportionate amount of the world's energy and resources. C. P. Snow's vision seems to become more realistic day by day—he foresaw the possibility of one-half of the world watching on color television while the other half starved to death.

What does this mean? What are we to do? The Jesus who placed the priority with the feeding of the hungry rather than with the preservation of an abstract law, leaves us little room to doubt what our priority should be. If we wish to feed the hungry, we must work for changes that affect the economic structure which allows such a disproportionate consumption. There are vast changes which must be made in the structure of our world economy. Our systems must be changed as numerous studies point out.[1]

In addition, however, each of us must get hold of hunger where we can and do what is best to ease it. We must exercise our own priorities. For example, if Americans substituted chicken for one-third of their beef consumption we could release enough grain to feed 100 million people every year.

Or, for example, if a pound of fertilizer from the 3 million tons which we use in America for non-food purposes (lawns and golf courses, etc.) could be transferred to Indian soil it would produce at least twice the additional yield as a pound of fertilizer on American soil.

Every church-going Christian in America has, through church channels, a means of concrete response to the world's hunger. The Christian can not only face this problem, he can help solve it.

3. CONSTRUCTION

The construction which emerges most naturally from this concern builds on the Epistle.

1. God has faced us in Jesus Christ.
2. Therefore, we can face God . . .
3. And face the world.

The OT and Gospel lessons come to bear especially on the third point.

1. See James A. Scherer, *Global Living Here and Now* (New York: Friendship Press, 1974).

The Third Sunday after Pentecost

Lutheran	Roman Catholic	Episcopal	Pres./UCC/Chr.	Methodist/COCU
Gen. 3:9–15	Gen. 3:9–15	Gen. 3:9–15	Gen. 3:9–15	Gen. 3:9–15
2 Cor. 4:13–5:1	2 Cor. 4:13–5:1	2 Cor. 4:13–5:1	2 Cor. 4:13–5:1	2 Cor. 4:13–5:1
Mark 3:20–35	Mark 3:20–35	Mark 3:20–35	Mark 3:20–35	Mark 3:20–35

EXEGESIS

Gospel: Mark 3:20–35. The text finds its place in the second main part of the Gospel (3:7–6:29). The immediate context encompasses the following units: the massive summary-passage describing Jesus' ministry in Galilee (3:7–12); the story of the choosing of the twelve (3:13–19); the text itself, which highlights sayings of Jesus concerning his alleged collusion with Satan (3:22–30) and his true family (3:20–21, 31–35); and Jesus' discourse in parables (4:1–34). Though a distinct unit, one purpose of the text is to prepare the reader for the parabolic speech to follow (cf. 3:23 to 4:2; 3:34 to 4:11).

The pericope on Jesus' true kindred (vv. 20–21, 31–35) forms a bracket around the pericope entitled "On Collusion with Satan" (vv. 22–30). This is a literary device of which Mark is fond (cf., e.g., 5:21–43; 11:12–25; 14:54–72) and indicates that the two pericopes are in some sense related. In this case, the unifying factor is the theme of "madness": the family of Jesus believes that he is mad mentally (v. 21), whereas the scribes believe that he is mad theologically (v. 22).

Mark records that Jesus goes home (v. 20a). A crowd gathers, with the result that he and his disciples are not able to eat (v. 20b–c). Meanwhile, news of Jesus' public activity has reached his family (v. 21; cf. 3:7–12). They think he is mad, so they leave home to seize him (v. 21). At this juncture the story breaks off.

The intervening scene describes Jesus in conflict with scribes from Jerusalem (vv. 22–30). The mere fact that these scribes are identified with Jerusalem is sufficient already to characterize them as being inimical to Jesus, for Jerusalem is the place where he will suffer and die (10:32–34). The scribes level a double charge against him: he is possessed of an unclean spirit and guilty of casting out demons by means of the prince of demons (vv. 22, 30). In reaction to the double charge, which reveals the scribes to be perverse and blind, Jesus addresses them in parables, that is, in speech they do not comprehend, in this way confirming their blindness (v. 23; 4:11–12). He asserts that it is absurd to accuse him of being in league with Satan, for Satan would then be at war with himself (vv. 24–26). On the contrary, he is "mightier" than the "strong man" Satan (v. 27; 1:7). God has endowed him with the Spirit so that the power of the kingdom is at work in him (1:10, 15). In driving out demons, he is releasing people from the bondage of Satan's rule, thus "plundering Satan's house," or kingdom (v. 27). In principle, God stands ready to forgive humans all their sins (v. 28). The one exception, however, is that one willfully and knowingly declare the Spirit's activity in him, the Son of God, to be "satanic" (vv. 29–30; 1:10–11). The scribes, therefore, had better beware.

With this, Mark returns to his story concerning the family of Jesus (vv. 31–35). They arrive at the house where Jesus is staying and send word, summoning him outside (v. 31). Upon hearing that his family stands without, Jesus looks searchingly at his followers seated around him (vv. 32–34a). Then, in solemn tones he announces that it is not his blood relatives as such who are his real mother and brother and sister, but those who do the will of God, that is to say, those who become his disciples (vv. 33b–35).

To conclude, the essential point of this text is that only the disciples of Jesus, those who follow him, can penetrate the mystery of his person, viz., that in him God is at work in the Spirit to rescue humans from Satan and all evil and to bring them into the gracious sphere of his rule. "Outsiders," on the other hand, contemplate the person and activity of Jesus and think him mad.

First Lesson: Gen.3:9–15. The whole of chap. 3 is of the nature of an aetiological legend explaining the origin of sin and the consequences of the fall. It is with the latter that the text has to do.

The fall of the man and of the woman into sin is described in 3:6: the woman plucks fruit from the tree of the knowledge of good and evil and eats, and the man takes from her. What motivates them is the thought that by eating this fruit they will suddenly possess the capacity to know everything. Their intention, therefore, is to expand the horizons of their existence beyond the limits set for them by God, which is rebellion against him.

Instead of increasing in wisdom, however, the man and the woman experience the results of sin described in the text. Thus, when the man hears God in the garden calling to him, he flees for fear because, he says, he is naked (vv. 9–10). In Israel, to appear naked before God was an abomination, expressly forbidden in connection with the cult (Exod.

20:26). In the text, nakedness connotes the shame the man feels towards both God and another human being (3:21). In addition, the man is afraid, and so flees from God (v. 10). Consequently, it is fear and shame, according to the text, that are the elemental symptoms of guilt.

Interrogated by God as to what he has done, the man blames the woman (vv. 11–12) and the woman blames the serpent (v. 13). Harmonious relationships have been destroyed. The text closes with the curse that God pronounces upon the serpent (vv. 14–15). This curse offers at once an ancient explanation of the physical make-up and of the behavior of the serpent (v. 14) and characterizes the species as emblematic of the evil with which the man must forever struggle without hope of victory (v. 15).

Theologically, the story of the fall prepares the worshiper for the word concerning forgiveness which is sounded in the Gospel for the day (Mark 3:28).

Second Lesson: 2 Cor. 4:13–5:1. As was the case with the Second Lesson appointed for Pentecost 2, Paul, in writing in the first person plural ("we"), is reflecting above all on his own situation. The immediate context is 4:7–5:10, and the principal subject under discussion is Paul's ministry.

In 4:7–12, Paul has argued that he, frail "earthenware vessel" that he is, has been entrusted with the "treasure" that is the gospel. Developing this theme, Paul declares in the text that the reason he proclaims, or "speaks," the gospel is that the same spirit who engendered faith in the Psalmist of old and so impelled him to speak has engendered faith in him (v. 13). Indeed, he proclaims the gospel in the manner he does because he is firmly convinced that God, who raised Jesus from the dead, will likewise raise up both him and the Corinthian Christians, so that together they will, with Jesus, triumphantly stand in the presence of God (v. 14). In point of fact, all the things Paul has been discussing, viz., his suffering (vv. 8–13), his faith, and his preaching, have but one purpose to serve: the benefit of the Corinthians (v. 15a). And what results as the grace of God supplies their every need is that it causes thanksgiving to abound to the glory of God (v. 15b).

Therefore, says Paul, he does not become tired and consequently neglect his duty (v. 16a). Because although the natural man is wasting away, day by day the spiritual man is being renewed (v. 16b–c). Present affliction is, after all, "light," and produces to an extraordinary degree an eternal "weight" of glory (v. 17). For this reason, he keeps his eyes fixed, not on the things seen but on the things unseen (v. 18). In the last analysis, his ultimate hope is rooted in the sure knowledge that should his earthly body be destroyed by either death or the second coming of Christ, he will receive from God a new, imperishable body (cf. 1 Cor. 15:51–57).

The Scripture readings for Pentecost 3 combine to set forth the following thought: in Christ, God forgives man his sin, enables him to do his will, and gives him a sure hope that will sustain him no matter what he encounters in life.

HOMILETICAL INTERPRETATION

1. CONCERN

In Christ, God forgives us our sin, enables us to do his will and gives us a sure hope.

2. CONFIRMATIONS AND CONCRETIONS

"Sin" seems to be an ugly little word that moderns want to hide away. The reality of it, however, is not so easily disposed of. The psychiatrist, Karl Menninger, asks boldly, "Whatever became of sin?"[1] The psychiatrist discovers that we violate moral boundaries even while trying to ignore them at terrible costs to ourselves.

"Whatever became of Adam?" might also be asked. The notion of an objective individual whose sin is genetically transmitted to the human race would get little support today, but the reality of the human condition symbolized in Adam's fall is inescapable. Sin is not just the acts we commit but the persons we are. Sin has to do with the communities in which we have our personal existence. Sin is a function of our social inheritance as well as of our choices. The modern man who looks for Adam need not search for the location of a garden in the ancient Near East. He should look instead at Washington, Los Angeles, New York, or, preferably, in his own mirror. The story of Adam and Eve continues to have power because it is the story of our lives. We transgress the moral boundaries and find ourselves expelled from paradise.

When the Lehman Wing of the Metropolitan Museum of Modern Art in New York City opened recently, thousands of persons saw a classic expression of this theme in Giovanni di Paolo's "Expulsion from Paradise," one of the fifteenth century treasures in that collection. Adam and Eve are seen hastening from the garden obviously very embarrassed. God hovers over them, unmistakably pointing the way out. That gesture may be said to sum up the OT lesson today.

1. Karl Menninger, *Whatever Became of Sin?* (New York: Hawthorn Books, 1973, 1974).

The NT lesson, however, might be summed up by the gesture of Jesus beckoning everyone to come unto him for forgiveness. The Gospel lesson assures us that all sins will be forgiven except the sin against the Holy Spirit. That sin, presumably, would be the denial of the power of God's Spirit to forgive sin.

The thanks which Jesus got for offering forgiveness, as recorded in the Gospel for today, was to be called "crazy." It is "mad" to believe that this Jesus can forgive us our sins and yet it is the "madness of God."[2] The forgiveness of our sins opens the way to do God's will and to hope for glory. The theme of the Epistle lesson is beautifully developed in a sermon by C. S. Lewis entitled "The Weight of Glory".[3]

Another useful resource in this area is the book *Images of Hope* by William S. Lynch.[4] Father Lynch has written a poetic and practical book which effectively links imagination and reality. The book was written out of conversations with psychiatrists and patients under psychiatric care. The author relates hope not only to our ultimate future, but to "The City of Man." He writes:

> "We can decide to build a human city, a city of man, in which all men have citizenship, Greek, Jew, and Gentile, the black and the white, the maimed, the blind, the mentally well and the mentally ill. This will always require an active imagination which will extend the idea of the human and which will imagine nothing in man it cannot contain."[5]

Hope is one of the most practical assets anyone can have.

3. CONSTRUCTION

The construction of this sermon follows the development of the concern in the sequence of the lessons.

    1. Fall (OT lesson).

    2. Forgiveness (Gospel lesson).

    3. Fulfillment (Second Lesson).

---

2. Cf. Elie Wiesel, *Zalman or the Madness of God* (New York: Random House, 1974) for a study of this theme in a Jewish context. Wiesel has offered a powerful story which argues that it is mad today to believe in God and in man. He urges us, however, to be mad.
3. Lewis, C. S., *The Weight of Glory* (Grand Rapids, Mich.: Eerdmans, 1965). See Roger Lancelyn Green and Walter Hooper, *C. S. Lewis: A Biography* (London: Collins, 1974) pp. 203-204.
4. William Lynch, S. J., *"Images of Hope: Imagination as Healer of the Hopeless"* (New York and Toronto: The New American Library, 1965).
5. Ibid., p. 21.

The Fourth Sunday after Pentecost

Lutheran	*Roman Catholic*	*Episcopal*	*Pres./UCC/Chr.*	*Methodist/COCU*
Ezek. 17:22–24	Ezek. 17:22–24	Ezek. 17:22–24	Ezek. 17:22–24	Ezek. 17:22–24
2 Cor. 5:6–10	2 Cor. 5:6–10	2 Cor. 5:6–10	2 Cor. 5:6–10	2 Cor. 5:6–10
Mark 4:26–34	Mark 4:26–34	Mark 4:26–34	Mark 4:26–34	Mark 4:26–34

EXEGESIS

Gospel: Mark 4:26–34. The text comprises the latter part of Jesus' discourse in parables (4:1–34). Both the seed growing secretly (vv. 26–29) and the mustard seed (vv. 30–32) are parables of the kingdom and therefore, to the eyes of faith, provide insight into the mystery of God's rule (v. 11).

The seed growing secretly and the mustard seed are what are known as companion, or double, parables. This means that though the message of each may differ, the two are similar in structure and content. Common to these parables are the features of contrast and growth.

In the parable of the seed growing secretly, reference is made to both seedtime (v. 26) and harvest (v. 29). This suggests contrast. The emphasis, however, does not lie here but on the element of growth (vv. 27–28): once the seed has been planted, the process of maturation begins, and "of itself" moves inexorably to completion. So it is, claims Mark, with the kingdom of God. In the person of Jesus of Nazareth, God has brought his rule to mankind (1:15); presently, in the time following Easter, he is unremittingly at work in the resurrected Jesus (cf. 14:28; 16:6–7) ordering the course of events (cf. 13:10) to the end that, at Jesus' parousia, he will establish his rule over all the world in majesty and splendor (8:38; 9:1; 13:24–27). As for the Christians of Mark's church, the message of this parable strengthens them in their belief that God, in the crucified and resurrected Jesus, is indeed in control of things, guiding them unswervingly towards the establishment in splendor of his end-time kingdom.

To turn to the parable of the mustard seed, the importance of the elements of contrast and of growth is the opposite of what we found in the parable of the seed growing secretly. While the element of growth is indeed present (vv. 31b–32a–c), the stress is on the element of contrast (vv. 31a, 32d). To make this clear, Mark has enclosed the key words "which is the smallest of all the seeds" (v. 31) in verbal brackets by having the same clause, but in reverse word-order, both precede and follow them: "whenever it is sown on the earth . . . on the earth, and whenever it is sown . . ." (vv. 31–32a). Thus, the thought of the parable is that the mustard seed, which was proverbial among the Jews as the smallest of quantities, grows up and miraculously becomes a tree in which the birds of the air can nest. Again, so it is, says Mark, with the kingdom of God. From such insignificant beginnings as the ministry of Jesus of Nazareth there will one day issue that splendid kingdom which will embrace all the nations of the world (cf. Dan. 4:1–12; Ezek. 17:23; 31:6). Accordingly, this parable, too, contains a message of confidence for the Christians of Mark's church.

The point of vv. 33–34 is that whereas the parables of Jesus strike "them," that is, the "outsiders" such as the Jewish crowds (cf. v. 2), as riddles, the "insiders," those who follow Jesus (cf. 4:11), are told their meaning. Applied to today, these verses set forth the basic Christian truth that genuine insight into the mystery of the kingdom is possible only by God-given faith in Jesus Christ.

First Lesson: Ezek. 17:22–24. Chap. 17 contains the allegories of the eagles (vv. 1–21) and of the cedar (vv. 22–24).

In the allegory of the eagles, Ezekiel reviews and evaluates events surrounding 588 B.C. Thus, Nebuchadnezzar, king of Babylon ("a great eagle," v. 3), had marched on Jerusalem ("Lebanon," v. 3) a decade earlier and had taken Jehoiachin ("the topmost of its young twigs," v. 4) captive, deporting him to Babylon ("land of trade," v. 4). In his place he had left Zedekiah ("seed of the land," v. 5) as a vassal king. Now, however, Zedekiah has decided to join forces with Pharaoh ("another great eagle," v. 7) in order to gain freedom from Babylon (v. 7), thus breaking his treaty with Nebuchadnezzar. Using the allegorical mode to speak out against Zedekiah, Ezekiel contends that Zedekiah's breach of treaty is tantamount to rebellion against God (v. 19). What will finally come of it, he predicts, is deportation to Babylon for Zedekiah and death for his army (vv. 20–21).

In contrast to this message of doom, the allegory of the cedar (vv. 22–24) is a word of promise. In place of the king of Babylon, Ezekiel describes God himself as choosing one from the house of David ("a tender shoot," v. 22; cf. Isa. 11:1; 53:2) and establishing him upon Mt. Zion ("a high and lofty mountain," v. 22). This son of David will become a mighty ruler ("a noble cedar," v. 23), and to him all who need help will look for protection ("birds of every kind," v. 23). Then, too, as they gaze upon him, all the kings of the world ("all the trees of the field," v. 24) will know that it is none other than God who humbles the mighty and exalts the lowly (v. 24; cf. Isa. 2:2–4; Luke 1:52).

While the OT writer did not, of course, have Jesus in mind when he told the allegory of the cedar, from a Christian standpoint it is in him that this allegory ultimately reached its fulfillment. Jesus, crucified and resurrected, is that one in the line of David whom God has made regent in the sphere of his rule.

Second Lesson: 2 Cor. 5:6–10. We recall that Paul has been speaking of the ministry and of the gospel entrusted to him (4:5, 7). He has referred to himself as an "earthenware vessel" (4:7) and depicted his sufferings (4:8–12). Starting with 4:16, however, he has begun to look to the future and talks of his hope (4:16–5:5). In the text he describes his person in the light of this hope.

Paul states that if he were to have his way, he would prefer to remain alive until the parousia of Christ, that is, until that time when his body will be changed and his mortal nature will put on immortality (5:4; cf. 1 Cor. 15:51–56). As the first step in the realization of this hope of future life, God has bestowed on him the gift of the Spirit (5:5).

Accordingly, Paul continues in the text, he is supremely confident (v. 6a), regardless of whether he should live or die. So long as he lives, he is separated, as it were, from Christ, who is at the right hand of God (v. 6b). Separated from the exalted Christ, he must walk by faith, without the capacity to see him (v. 7). But should he die, he would be at home with the Lord (v. 8). Still, either way his one goal is to be obedient to Christ, for the disciple is utterly responsible to him and must one day give him account for his life on earth (vv. 9–10).

HOMILETICAL INTERPRETATION

1. CONCERN

The Christian walks by faith in the confidence that history finds its fulfillment in Jesus Christ.

2. CONFIRMATIONS AND CONCRETIONS

Faith in a simple or "animal" sense is basic to human life. Without faith we would have to examine the floor every morning before getting out of bed, have our car checked before driving it, and do an interrogation of every individual before talking with him further.

To say that we walk by faith is to describe a simple condition of human life. However, when the author of the Epistle to the Corinthians wrote, "We walk by faith, not by sight" he was referring to faith in Jesus Christ—faith far more radical and demanding than mere "animal" faith.

This is the faith in Jesus Christ which issues in the confidence that however much our life on earth may seem an exile, we do have an ultimate destination. This faith issues in courage. The word the author of the Epistle uses is a form of *Tharrēo*. The RSV translates this as "courage" in place of the King James' "confidence," and courage seems the more accurate word for the original carries the meaning of boldness and daring. Faith in Christ gives us such daring.

John F. Kennedy, while a Senator, wrote a book entitled *Profiles in Courage*. The book is about moral courage on the part of parliamentary leaders who because of principle confront the opposition of colleagues, constituents, and a majority of the general public. The book contains many examples worth study including James W. Grimes who cast one of the deciding votes of "not guilty" in regard to the impeachment of President Andrew Johnson. Because of his stand, Grimes was burned in effigy, accused by the press of "idiocy and impotency," and repudiated by his state and friends. His political career never recovered but before he died, he declared to a friend:

> "I shall ever thank God that in that troubled hour of trial, when many privately confessed that they had sacrificed their judgment and their conscience at the behest of party newspapers and party-hate, I had the courage to be true to my oath and my conscience . . ."[1]

Such courage does not always mean that the possessor of it is in the right. Yet, our parliamentary system could not exist at all if it were not for persons of courage who were able to put what they believed to be right above the pressures of the immediate. And courage, wherever we find it, is in the long run one of the most compelling of human virtues.

Courage is also one of the most essential qualities. Paul Tillich has emphasized the courage to be as the act by which a person affirms himself in the face of all the uncertainties and anxieties of life.[2]

Christian faith affirms that God is at work even where it is not obvious, just as we have confidence that a seed is growing even when it is hidden in the ground.

We are called to labor wherever we can; to participate in the kingdom of God. There may be little recognition and less applause for our acts to allay wounds and heal the hurts in our complex society. We may often

1. John F. Kennedy, *Profiles in Courage* (New York: Pocketbooks, 1957), p. 128.
2. See Paul Tillich, *The Courage to Be* (New Haven: Yale University Press, 1952).

work alone or seem to, but our faith in God gives us confidence to take the next step. That one step by faith may lead us nearer our ultimate destination than the many circuitous steps which lead us away from our immediate responsibilities in our daily lives.

3. CONSTRUCTION

These passages suggest a doctrinal sermon on faith:

1. The introduction would deal with the definition of faith as distinguished from "animal" faith and would draw heavily on the Second Lesson.
2. A major portion of the sermon should be the development of faith as courage.
3. Another major portion of the sermon should deal with faith as confidence, the assurance that God is at work even when we may not be aware of it.

The Fifth Sunday after Pentecost

Lutheran	Roman Catholic	Episcopal	Pres./UCC/Chr.	Methodist/COCU
Job 38:1–11	Job 38:1, 8–11	Job 38:1–11, 16–18	Job 38:1–11	Job 38:1–11, 16–18
2 Cor. 5:14–17	2 Cor. 5:14–17	2 Cor. 5:14–17	2 Cor. 5:16–21	2 Cor. 5:14–17
Mark 4:35–41	Mark 4:35–40	Mark 4:35–41	Mark 4:35–41	Mark 4:35–41

EXEGESIS

Gospel: Mark 4:35–41. The text begins a section of the Gospel in which Jesus and the disciples are depicted as undertaking six voyages back and forth across the Sea of Galilee (4:35–8:21; cf. 4:35; 5:1, 21; 6:45; 8:13). In this way Jesus is pictured as discharging his ministry among both Jews and Gentiles.

Mark writes that towards evening on the day on which Jesus has delivered his parabolic discourse to the crowd (4:1–34), he summons his disciples to go with him to the other side of the lake (v. 35). The disciples dismiss the crowd and, in the company of other vessels, embark with Jesus on the voyage (v. 36; cf. 4:1). Out on the lake, a fierce squall suddenly arises, and the boat of Jesus and the disciples is in danger of being swamped by the waves (v. 37). Jesus, at peace, is asleep in the stern of the boat, but the disciples, afraid, arouse him with the reproach: "Teacher, do you not care if we perish?" (v. 38). Awakened, Jesus rebukes the wind and the sea with the words, "Be silent, be muzzled," and at his command the wind abates, giving way to a great calm (v. 39). Then Jesus turns on the disciples and asks them why they are so cowardly and lacking in faith (v. 40). The disciples, who receive Jesus' question with fear and hence incomprehension, can only look at one another and ask who he might be, that even wind and sea obey him (v. 41).

Several features of this miracle-story are of weighty theological significance. Thus, Jesus commands the wind and the sea with the same word ("be muzzled") with which he casts out demons (1:25). This and the great calm that ensues are reminiscent of God's power over the waters of chaos at the creation (Pss. 74:13–14; 104:5–9; Job 38:8–11; Jer. 5:22). Mark, then, portrays Jesus in this story as the one whom God has invested with divine authority and who consequently has control over the demonic forces of nature. Therefore it is in the question the disciples pose in v. 41 that the narrative reaches its climax: Who, exactly, is Jesus? In the succeeding paragraph, Mark provides the answer: He is the almighty Son of God (5:7; cf. 1:23–27; 3:11).

The disciples in the story are said to be cowardly, without faith, and fearful (vv. 40–41). Instead of being like Jesus, who, at peace in the care of his Father, sleeps in the midst of the storm, they are without the courage of faith and so awaken Jesus in order to reproach him for not being concerned about their welfare (v. 38). Furthermore, the fact that they react with fear to Jesus' admonition of their cowardice and lack of faith (v. 41) discloses that they have failed to grasp the significance of the miracle and therefore of the person of Jesus. Hence, this story, too, reflects the familiar Markan theme of persistent ignorance on the part of the disciples about the mystery of Jesus' person and work (cf. 6:52; 8:17, 21; 9:6, 32).

As he directs this pericope at the Christians of his church, one thing Mark does is to use the negative example of the disciples to proclaim faith in the all powerful Son of God. In him these Christians are to find courage to withstand the vicissitudes of life.

First Lesson: Job 38:1–11. The Book of Job is not unlike a Greek tragedy. In it, the protagonist is made to ask a question that is innate to life itself: Why must a human being endure suffering? The fact that Job is characterized at the outset as a "blameless and upright man" (chaps. 1–2) only makes the question more acute.

At the conclusion of his dialogues with Eliphaz, Bildad, and Zophar (chaps. 3–31), Job boldly reviews his past behavior in order to assert his moral innocence before God and his fellows (chap. 31). Indeed, at this point Job challenges God to meet with him and to argue with him his case (31:35–37). In two discourses at the end of the book, God meets Job's challenge (38:1–40:5; 40:6–42:6).

Taken together, these discourses of God, of which the text is a portion, comprise the dramatic and theological high point of the book. Dramatically, following the inconclusive counsel of Job's friends, the scene is set for God to deliver the final word. And theologically, in speaking with Job, God gives answer to his question.

The text states that God addresses Job from a "whirlwind" (v. 1), which is a common setting in the OT for divine appearances, or theophanies (cf. Ps. 50:3; Ezek. 1:4; Nah. 1:3; Zech. 9:14). But although Job believes that his innocence entitles him to call God to account, God immediately makes it clear that he has come to call Job to account (vv. 2–3).

In essence, God's answer to Job's question about suffering is the revelation that he, who is the author of all creation, cannot be comprehended in his ways by human beings. Hence, the final resolution of the problem of righteous suffering must be seen to lie hidden in the mystery of his divine person.

To convey this message to Job, God overawes him in the text with a description of two acts of creation. Referring to his creation of the world, God pictures the earth as a building so gigantic that he alone can know its make-up and dimensions (vv. 4–7). And referring to his creation of the seas, God gives illustration of his limitless power: calling forth the "cosmic birth" of the waters of the world, he has clothed them with clouds and darkness and has prescribed for them their boundaries (vv. 8–11). Appropriately, Job responds to God's words to him by taking cognizance of his smallness and by stilling his tongue (40:3–5).

The text complements the Gospel especially with regard to the second illustration: the power of God to create and control the waters of the world manifests itself in the Son of God, whom both sea and wind obey.

Second Lesson: 2 Cor. 5:14–17. The text's wider context is 2:14–7:4, and its immediate context is 5:11–21. The broad objective of Paul in the former is to treat of his ministry and its purpose, and he accomplishes this in the latter by discussing the message of reconciliation. The focus of the text itself is on the "new creation" that arises out of the death and resurrection of Christ.

Using the editorial "we," Paul declares in the text that his person and his actions are governed by one thing only, viz., the love that Christ has shown him in the cross (v. 14a). The reason Christ's love controls him is that his death on the cross is of benefit for all mankind (cf. 1 Cor. 15:3): when he died, all people died (v. 14b–d). How is this to be understood? In Christ's death all people died in the sense that, when appropriated by faith, this death releases people from the necessity to lead a life that is centered on the self and frees them to lead a life that finds its center in him, the One crucified and resurrected (v. 15; cf. Rom. 6:1–14).

Of course, continues Paul, a death of this sort is of enormous consequence for daily life. Thus, negatively speaking, the shape of one's existence is no longer determined by purely human values and standards (v. 16a). In this respect, consider even Christ. Once he was seen solely as a human being (v. 16b). But he is not now so to be regarded, for he is the resurrected and exalted Lord (v. 16c).

From a positive standpoint, the result of dying with Christ is that one thereafter is "in Christ" and therefore a "new creation," viz., one lives in this age as one who, by faith in Christ, has already passed through death and resurrection and so is a member of the glorious age to come (v. 17a–b; Gal. 2:20). For such a one, the old, self-centered way of relating to the world is gone; it has been replaced by the new, Christ-centered way (v. 17c–d).

In relation to the Gospel for the day, Paul's description of the new being in Christ is the gospel-counterpart to the negative example the disciples set in Mark. On this score, this text is the necessary balance to that one.

HOMILETICAL INTERPRETATION

1. Concern

The power of God to create and control the waters of the world manifests itself in the Son of God, whom both sea and wind obey, and in the creation of the new being.

2. Confirmations and Concretions

The Board of Trustees of a college once appointed a committee to install a heating unit in the administration building. The new heater was installed but the heating problem was not solved. For it was then discovered that the pipes were inadequate to handle the heat produced by the new unit. The entire system had to be replaced.

Something like this occurs when Christ comes alive for us. We may wish that that new center of energy might fit easily into the apparatus of our old conveniences and desires. We soon discover, however, that a whole new system is demanded. "If anyone is in Christ he is a new creation: The old is passed away, behold, the new has come."

Writers know the importance of the point of view. Every story has to be written from a certain P.O.V., as it is sometimes called. That determines everything else in the story. The writer of 2 Corinthians knows that basic to the new being is a new point of view. We don't look at anyone from a human point of view any longer but from the point of view which comes with Christ.

Indeed we do not look *at* Christ any longer. That is, Christ is not an object totally outside us, a figure for historical investigation. We are, rather, *in* Christ. We actually participate in the new being he brought. This is the complete antithesis of the "playing" with Christ which we have spoken of earlier. We do not "play" with Christ, we *participate in* Christ.

This new being is a gift, a gift from God through Christ. "God was in Christ reconciling the world to himself, not counting their trespasses against them, and entrusting to us the message of reconciliation"—surely this is one of the greatest lines of Scripture.[1]

The new being in Christ does not mean that we are not troubled. Indeed our sensitivities are heightened and we may be more anguished than before. The message of Job, therefore, is not to be dismissed.[2]

The Gospel lesson is also relevant here because even the disciple of Christ will find himself in rough waters and that is a threatening experience. Rembrandt gave it a classic expression in his painting of "The Calming of the Sea" which may be found in The Isabella Stewart Gardner Museum in Boston. The different reactions of the disciples are depicted with painful detail: We see one clutching the mast, another leaning over the side of the boat. Christ, however, remains secure and asleep. There is a radiance about his calm which suggests the power with which he will soon calm the sea.

3. CONSTRUCTION

These texts suggest a sermon on the new being with three major sections each dealing with one of the lessons for the day.

1. Being New (Second Lesson).
2. Being Troubled (the OT lesson).
3. Being Calm (the Gospel).

1. See especially Donald Baillie, *God was in Christ* (New York: Scriptures, 1948).
2. See especially Archibald MacLeish, *J. B.: A Play in Verse* (Boston: Houghton Mifflin, 1958), and Robert Frost, *A Masque of Reason* (New York: Holt, 1945).

The Sixth Sunday after Pentecost

Lutheran	Roman Catholic	Episcopal	Pres./UCC/Chr.	Methodist/COCU
Lam. 3:22–33	Wisd. 1:13–15; 2:23–35	Wisd. 1:13–15; 2:23–24	Gen. 4:3–10	Lam. 3:22–23
2 Cor. 8:1–9, 13–14	2 Cor. 8:7, 9, 13–15	2 Cor. 8:1–9, 13–15	2 Cor. 8:7–15	2 Cor. 8:1–9, 13–15
Mark 5:21–24a, 35–43 *or*	Mark 5:21–43 *or*	Mark 5:21–24, 35b–43	Mark 5:21–43	Mark 5:21–43
Mark 5:24b–34	Mark 5:21–24, 35b–43			

EXEGESIS

Gospel: Mark 5:21–24a, 35–43. The text, the story of the raising of Jairus' daughter, is one of four miracles Mark associates with Jesus' first voyage to the eastern, or Gentile, side of the Sea of Galilee (4:35–5:20) and his return to the western, or Jewish, side (5:21–43). Literarily, it surrounds the story of the healing of a woman with a hemorrhage (5:25–34). Earlier we encountered this same compositional device (cf. 3:20–25: vv. 20–21, 22–30, 31–35), and noted that it indicates that the units so combined are closely related to each other. In this case, the relatedness is in terms of structure, since both units are miracle stories, and of content, since there is in both an emphasis on the dual themes of restoration (cf. vv. 29, 34 to v. 42) and of faith (cf. v. 34 to v. 36).

Mark writes that when Jesus returns to the western shore of the Sea of Galilee, a great crowd gathers around him (v. 21). There beside the sea, Jairus, who is either the president of the local synagogue or one of its seven leaders, approaches him, falls down in homage before him, and fervently pleads with him that he should come and place his hands on his sick daughter so that she might be healed and live (vv. 22–23). Jesus goes with him (v. 24a).

Because Jesus is delayed on the way to Jairus' house by a woman who has suffered from hemorrhages and whom he heals (vv. 24b–34), news reaches Jairus that his daughter no longer lives (v. 35). Though the situation now appears hopeless, Jesus ignores the report and exhorts Jairus to cast aside fear and doubt and to believe (v. 36). Later, taking with him Peter, James, and John, Jesus enters the house of Jairus, only to encounter mass confusion, with people (perhaps professional mourners) weeping and wailing loudly (vv. 37–38). Seeing this, Jesus asks the mourners why they are so distressed and weeping, and tells them that the girl is not dead but merely sleeping (v. 39). The mourners reply with ridicule, for to them the girl is beyond help (v. 40a). Jesus, however, expels them from the house, and then ushers his three disciples and the parents into the room where the girl is lying (v. 40b–c). Taking her by the hand, Jesus bids the girl in Aramaic to arise, and she responds at once, getting up and walking (vv. 41–42a). When the disciples and the parents witness this, absolute astonishment grips them, a sign that the "impossible" has in fact happened (v. 42). In addition, Jesus' command to silence likewise underlines the unique thing that has taken place, and the fact that the girl can eat is proof that she has indeed returned to life (v. 43).

For the Christians of Mark's church, this story bore the following message: the disciple of Jesus is to be like Jairus and in faith look to the resurrected Son of God for life and salvation; he it is who commands the very power of God which can break the bonds of death itself.

First Lesson: Lam. 3:22–33. Chap. 3 is a tripartite acrostic poem composed in such a way that in Hebrew each three verses begin with the same letter of the alphabet. The first main part is a psalm of personal distress ending on a note of praise (vv. 1–24); the second is paraenetic in content and counsels submission under affliction and penitence (vv. 25–51); and the third is a psalm that calls upon God for vindication and the requiting of the enemy (vv. 52–66). If vv. 34–36 and 43–48 can be pressed historically, the poem was written for Israelites for whom the invasion of their land and the destruction of Jerusalem (587 B.C.) were still a vivid memory. It may be that it had its place in the cult and was read at prescribed times to the gathered community.

The text overlaps parts one and two of the poem. The individual speaking is "the man" of v. 1, who regards himself as authorized to address the lamenting community because he, too, knows what it is to experience the judgment and wrath of God (vv. 1–3). Some commentators identify "the man" with Jeremiah, but this is unlikely.

Vv. 22–24 constitute a confessional hymn of thanksgiving that articulates the basis for renewed hope. Vv. 22–23 recall Exod. 34:6 and remind the suffering assembly that throughout the history of the covenant God has fundamentally revealed himself to be a God of love and mercy. The statement in v. 24, "The Lord is my portion," expresses the notion that God, just like the land from which and upon which one lives, is the true sustenance of every Israelite.

The second three verses of the text enjoin the community to patience in the present time of affliction. The key word in them is "good." Because God is "kind," or good (v. 25), so it is "good" for humans to submit to his will and quietly await his salvation (vv. 26–27).

The third section counsels the community not to resign itself to suffering, but willingly to accept it (vv. 28–30). For, declares the speaker in
the final three verses of the text, God, because he is loving by nature and
not wrathful, will not "cast off" his own forever but will look upon their
"grief" and visit them with his compassion (vv. 31–33).

In line with the Gospel reading, the text calls Christians to patience
and hope in times of affliction. Such an attitude springs from trust in the
God who in his Son has destroyed the power of death.

Second Lesson: 2 Cor. 8:1–9, 13–14. While Paul makes mention in
no fewer than four of his letters of the collection he was gathering among
the Gentile churches for the Jewish Christians in Jerusalem, nowhere does
he discuss this more extensively than in 2 Cor. 8–9 (cf. Rom. 15:25–29;
1 Cor. 16:1–4; Gal. 2:10). Sketching the background of this collection
will shed light on the text.

The church that grew up in Jerusalem following Pentecost was im-
poverished from the outset (cf. Acts 6:1). Jewish hostility and persecution
only contributed to its financial plight (Acts 4:1–3; 5:17–18; 6:12–14;
8:1–3; 9:1–2; 12:1–3). At the same time, theologically this church was
suspicious of any mission to the Gentiles, believing that the Jews had
priority in God's plan of salvation (cf. Acts 10; 11:2–3).

In A.D. 40 or 41, a Jewish-Christian prophet from Jerusalem named
Agabus visited the church at Antioch and prophesied that famine was
about to engulf the world (Acts 11:27–28). Realizing the precarious
situation of the Christians in Jerusalem, the church in Antioch set about
gathering aid for them (Acts 11:29).

Between A.D. 40 and 48, a severe shortage of food did in fact develop
in Judea. In these same years, Paul also began concerted missionary work
among the Gentiles. By A.D. 48, the shape of events made it necessary
to convoke the so-called Apostolic Council. It convened in Jerusalem in
order to deal with the question of fellowship between Christians of Jewish
and of Gentile background (Acts 15:1–35; Gal. 2:1–10). But it also provided the occasion for Paul and Barnabas to bring to Jerusalem the relief
that the church at Antioch had finally gathered (Acts 11:30).

The outcome of the Apostolic Council was the emergence of two wings
within the early church: the Gentile wing, under Paul; and the Jewish
wing, under Peter, James, and John (Gal. 2:7–9). The latter, however,
urged Paul not to forget the poor in Jerusalem (Gal. 2:10).

Paul's collection among Gentile Christians originated with this plea.
He saw it as a means to maintain "fellowship" between the two branches
of the church (2 Cor. 8:4; 9:13) and to facilitate "equality" in the sense

that "those who have" might share their abundance with "those who have not" (2 Cor. 8:13–15). And the Gentile Christians, reasoned Paul, will be all the more pleased to contribute to their Jewish-Christian brothers because they are in debt to them for the gift of the gospel (Rom. 15:27).

In the text, Paul holds the Macedonians up as an example for the Corinthians to emulate in meeting their obligations for the collection (vv. 1–5). The thing to note, however, is that Paul motivates the collection theologically. In v. 5, he speaks of first giving oneself to the Lord, and in v. 9 he refers to God's grace in Christ. Paul's point is that it is response to God's love in Christ which produces true liberality towards the neighbor.

In conjunction, the three Scripture readings for the day suggest the following related thoughts: God, who reveals himself in Jesus Christ, is the Christian's hope in times of affliction; as the recipient of God's love, the Christian deals liberally with his neighbor.

HOMILETICAL INTERPRETATION

1. CONCERN

The disciple of Jesus Christ looks to the resurrected Son of God for life and salvation, trusting God in times of affliction and serving others.

2. CONFIRMATIONS AND CONCRETIONS

"There may yet be hope." This line from the OT lesson (Lam. 3:29) comes out of a desperate situation. It was written by one who may well have been an eyewitness to the fall of Jerusalem and to the destruction of the temple. A profound sense of grief is expressed throughout Lamentations as well as a sense of horror worthy of Ezekiel. The author is familiar with people who brood in silence. He has seen good people with their faces in the dust. But he believes "there may yet be hope," for the faithfulness of the Lord is "new every morning" (Lam. 3:22).

An important novel of recent years was entitled *Nectar in a Sieve*. It was the story of a woman in India whose life bore the double burden of poverty and sexual discrimination. Yet the theme of the book, from Samuel Taylor Coleridge, is that life without hope is like nectar in a sieve; for we cannot live without hope.

The author of Lamentations knew that. But even more he knew the authentic hope which finds the Lord as its source.

Such hope is put to a severe test in the face of death. Jesus' raising of the daughter of Jairus is a miracle or "wonder" which carries the message that the resurrected Christ brings hope even in hopeless situations. Death will appear to be an end. Anyone who has looked literally into the face of death would be forgiven that conclusion. Yet the testimony of faith, again and again, is that death is not an epilogue at the end of life, but an episode in endless life.

A good friend of mine suffered with his wife through a terrible illness. Yet they faced that suffering with faith. Later he said to me, "I have come to a new and deep understanding of the lines of the hymn, 'Those angel faces smile, which we have loved long since and lost awhile.' " His name was Edward. It could have been Jairus.

The author of the Epistle to the Corinthians did not hesitate to link his hopes with the stewardship of the hopeful. The Second lesson for today is a powerful plea for cheerful giving. The author assumes that the love of the Corinthians is real and asks that they express it in more than words. It is as if we are being reminded that Christians are to be not only the recipients of hope but the givers of hope. We are so to contribute our material resources that we may give hope to others—hope for the suffering, hope for the hungry, hope for the needy, hope for the desperate. The source of that giving is plainly God himself. He was rich but he became poor for us. Therefore, we are "to give and give and give again as God has given us."

3. CONSTRUCTION

There are two major ways of developing this concern. One is to prepare a doctrinal sermon on hope. Such a sermon might take the following outline:

    1. "There may yet be hope" (the OT lesson).
    2. Even in the face of death (the Gospel).
    3. When we share our resources we may get hope to others (Second Lesson).

Another possibility is to preach an expository sermon based on the Second lesson dealing with stewardship and making reference to the other lessons. Yet another possibility is to take the direction suggested by Lamentations and preach a sermon on "New Every Morning" which deals with the perpetual freshness of God's providence and which proceeds through treatment of the other lessons.

The Seventh Sunday after Pentecost

Lutheran	*Roman Catholic*	*Episcopal*	*Pres./UCC/Chr.*	*Methodist/COCU*
Ezek. 2:2–5	Ezek. 2:2–5	Ezek. 2:2–5	Ezek. 2:1–5	Ezek. 2:1–5
2 Cor. 12:7–10	2 Cor. 12:7–10	2 Cor. 12:7–10	2 Cor. 12:7–10	2 Cor. 12:7–10
Mark 6:1–6	Mark 6:1–6	Mark 6:1–6	Mark 6:1–6	Mark 6:1–6

EXEGESIS

Gospel: Mark 6:1–6. The story of the rejection of Jesus at Nazareth recalls the Gospel reading for Pentecost 3, which tells of Jesus' true family (Mark 3:21, 31–35). There the family of Jesus, reacting to his public activity (3:7–12), is portrayed as thinking him mad (3:21), with the result that they leave home to get him (3:21, 31–32). Instead of submitting to his family, however, Jesus looks around him at his followers and declares that his real mother and brother and sister are those who do the will of God (3:33–35). In other words, Jesus turns from his family and towards his followers.

If the Gospel for Pentecost 3 depicts Jesus' break with his family, the text depicts his break with the townspeople of Nazareth (vv. 1, 4), especially with his relatives (v. 4). In this case, too, the disciples are made to contrast sharply with those who oppose Jesus. Whereas the disciples are said to "follow" him (v. 1; cf. 1:16–20; 2:14–15; 8:34), the townspeople and relatives become "astonished" at his teaching (v. 2a–b) and "offended" by his wisdom and mighty works (vv. 2c–e, 3d). They know him to be a carpenter and are acquainted with his mother and brothers and sisters (v. 3a–c). Therefore in their view he is not to be attributed the divine dignity and authority to which his teaching and healing allude. As the conclusion to this pericope, v. 6a is most fitting, for the word "unbelief" shows clearly that the "astonishment" of the people and the "offense" they take at Jesus do indeed indicate a rejection on their part of his divine sonship as implied by his miracles or message of the kingdom (cf. 1:11, 14–15, 23–28, 32–34; 3:7–12).

V. 4 seems to imply that the title "prophet" is appropriate to Jesus. The saying, however, has the character of a proverb and possesses many parallels in Greek, Hellenistic, and Roman literature. It should not be pressed as a title of majesty for Jesus, because the Christology Mark develops in his Gospel is that of Son of God and Son of man. "Prophet" for Mark signifies no more than the way in which the populace regard both John the Baptist and Jesus (cf. 6:15; 8:27–28).

The strange comment in v. 5a, "And he could do no mighty work there . . . ," should not be taken to mean, as v. 5b plainly reveals, that Jesus was unable as such to perform a miracle. Instead, it is intended to call attention to the enormity of the unbelief of the townspeople of Nazareth and of the relatives of Jesus (v. 6).

One thing this text illustrates well is the challenge of faith with which Jesus confronts all who encounter him: Will one confess him to be the Son of God and follow him, or will one take offense at him and deny his claim to fealty?

First Lesson: Ezek. 2:2–5. In chap. 1, Ezekiel describes his vision of the glory of the Lord (c. 594 B.C.). In it God discloses to him that, Israel's deportation to Babylon notwithstanding (1:1), he is still the ruler of the universe (1:26–28). As such, he has determined, Ezekiel writes in the text, to declare his will to the exiles (2:4). For this purpose he calls (1:28b) and commissions (2:3–4) Ezekiel to be his prophetic mouthpiece to them (2:5).

God addresses Ezekiel in the text as "son of man" (v. 1). This designation is not to be confused with the use Jesus makes of it in the Gospels, for here it underlines the creatureliness and finitude of Ezekiel over against God (cf. Job 25:6; Ps. 8:4). In point of fact, for Ezekiel even to be able to stand upright and to converse with God it is necessary that God empower him with his Spirit (v. 2; cf. Job 34:14–15; Ps. 104:29–30).

Ezekiel receives his commission in vv. 3–4. Following the demise of the northern kingdom, Judah had proudly arrogated to itself the title "house of Israel." But this people, God announces to Ezekiel, has become a "house of rebellion" (v. 5). Accordingly, he is to go to them and fearlessly to proclaim in their midst the word of the Lord (vv. 3–4). Whether he succeeds or fails in his mission is to be of no concern to him (vv. 6–7). Regardless of how the people receive him, the decisive thing is that God's word will have sounded forth and "they will know that there has been a prophet among them" (vv. 4–5).

It should be recognized in passing that the true link between this text and the Gospel for the day is not to be found in the word "prophet" (cf. v. 5 to Mark 6:4) but in the theme of rejection and rebellion. Both Ezekiel and Jesus are sent to a "rebellious house."

Second Lesson: 2 Cor. 12:7–10. The congregation at Corinth had been invaded by Jewish Christians from Palestine of Gnostic-pneumatic stripe whom Paul terms in his letter "superlative apostles" (11:5; 12:11). These individuals have, on the one hand, cast aspersions upon the person (4:2; 5:11–12; 7:2; 10:2; 12:16), gospel (4:3; 13:3), ministry (6:3), and apostleship (3:1; 10:13–14; 12:12) of Paul, and, on the other, have boasted of their own credentials (3:1; 10:12, 18), position (5:12), mission (11:12, 18), apostleship (11:5; 12:11), and revelatory experiences (5:13; 12:1, 7). In chaps. 11–12, Paul suddenly turns the tables on them and bids the Corinthians to bear with him in a "little foolishness" (11:1). Specifically, he, too, will boast (11:16, 21; 12:1), but only of his weaknesses (11:21, 30; 12:5, 9). The text comprises four verses of Paul's exercise in "boastfulness."

If the "superlative apostles" are bent on boasting of their ecstasies, then Paul asserts in the text that he, no less than they, has also had an "abundance of revelations" (v. 7a; cf. 12:1–4). But because God did not want him to get a "swelled head" over them, he gave him a "thorn in the flesh," that is to say, a messenger of Satan, to beat him (v. 7). In prayer, Paul has earnestly and repeatedly pleaded with God to remove this from him (v. 8). But God's final answer is that the love he has shown him in Christ (8:9) is sufficient to sustain him, for it is in weakness that his divine power comes to its full strength (v. 9a–c; 4:7). In order, therefore, that the power of Christ may dwell within him, Paul is only too happy to boast of his weaknesses (v. 9d–e). For him it is a spiritual law: when he is weak, then he is strong (v. 10).

Paul's reference to a "thorn in the flesh" (v. 7) has elicited a welter of speculation. Some have reasoned that it was a physical or emotional malady, such as epilepsy (2 Cor. 12:7), hysteria, periodic depressions, headaches, eye-trouble (cf. Gal. 4:15), malaria, leprosy, or a speech impediment (cf. 2 Cor. 10:1, 9–10; 11:6). Others have argued that it was a spiritual affliction, such as temptation brought about by opponents or pangs of conscience. In the last analysis, the evidence is simply too meager to permit anything but the most calculated guess. Furthermore, one must remember that Paul's health was not so fragile that he could not endure the many hardships he lists in the text (v. 10) and elsewhere in his letters.

HOMILETICAL INTERPRETATION

1. CONCERN

The secret of the Christian's strength is that God's power is made perfect in his weakness. This "weakness" offends the unbeliever but sets the believer on his feet.

2. CONFIRMATIONS AND CONCRETIONS

Some people are "survivors." No matter how rough life gets they come through. Other people seem to wilt or be destroyed by relatively lighter demands. What is the secret strength of the survivor? For the Christian the secret of strength is to know one's weakness. "When I am weak, then I am strong" (2 Cor. 12:7–10). This is a paradox, but like all paradoxes in the end its truth proves out. To pretend that we are strong all the time is an invitation to disaster. To act as if we can be "on top" of every situation, "the master of all we survey," is to prepare ourselves for defeat.

Emily Dickinson once wrote about such people:

> How awful to be somebody,
> How public like a frog,
> To tell your name the livelong day
> To an admiring bog.

Such activity may be good public relations for a frog, but for a human it reveals insecurity, not strength.

Real strength comes from knowing that we do not have to be masters of every situation precisely because we know the One who is. Confident about God's strength, we can be humble about our own. That is the secret of survival.

Faith in God's power is an ingredient of strength. We know that his grace is sufficient for us. Helen Kim was the moving spirit behind the founding of the great Ewha University in Korea. The odds against her were enormous, but she created one of our great Christian institutions. When she told the story of her life she took as her title, *Grace Sufficient.*[1]

The prophet Ezekiel faced an overwhelming situation. An inventory of his own resources would have left him in despair, but he allowed the Spirit to enter into him and the Spirit set him on his feet. Ezekiel in his weakness let the mighty God speak through him. Therein lay the power of the prophet for Ezekiel and for ourselves.

Jesus himself appeared "weak" to many of his contemporaries. They were expecting a kind of Superman. They anticipated spectacular signs and unmistakable evidences of his divinity. They saw only a carpenter's son, a local boy, a prophet without honor. Yet all the power of God came to expression in that "weakness." The "weakness" of God proved mightier than the strength of men.

1. See *Grace Sufficient: The Story of Helen Kim by Herself,* edited by J. Manning Potts (Nashville: The Upper Room, 1964). Dr. Kim's Ph.D. dissertation is entitled "Rural Education for the Regeneration of Korea" (Columbia University, 1931).

How can we survive in difficult times? Through the paradox of strength —God's strength made perfect in our weakness.

3. CONSTRUCTION

The Epistle Lesson is a key stating the paradox of strength. The sermon could build from this, with an introduction exploring the paradox. The development of the meaning could be related to:

1. Ezekiel.
2. Jesus.
3. Ourselves.

The Eighth Sunday after Pentecost

Lutheran	Roman Catholic	Episcopal	Pres./UCC/Chr.	Methodist/COCU
Amos 7:10–15	Amos 7:12–15	Amos 7:10–15	Amos 7:12–17	Amos 7:10–15
Eph. 1:3–14	Eph. 1:3–14	Eph. 1:13–14	Eph. 1:3–10	Eph. 1:3–14
Mark 6:7–13	Mark 6:7–13	Mark 6:7–13	Mark 6:7–13	Mark 6:7–13

EXEGESIS

Gospel: Mark 6:7–13. The story of the commissioning of the twelve is one of a series of narratives (6:1–33) which Mark has inserted between two cycles of miracle-stories (4:35–5:43; 6:32–56). The first narrative of this series is Jesus' rejection in Nazareth (6:1–6), which is the Gospel reading for Pentecost 7. Next comes the text, which finds its logical conclusion in Mark's report of the return of the disciples and hence forms a bracket around the pericope on the death of John the Baptist (6:7–13, 14–29, 30–31).

Mark states that Jesus, following his rejection in Nazareth, goes around among the villages teaching (v. 6b). Then he summons the twelve and sends them out, giving them instructions about their mission (vv. 7–11). A terse description of this mission concludes the pericope (vv. 12–13).

The twin facts that Jesus is portrayed as teaching in the villages around Nazareth (v. 6b) and that mention is made of the twelve (v. 7a) indicate that the missionary journey of the disciples is to Israel. The Greek verb translated "to send out" (v. 7a) emphasizes the circumstance that the disciples carry out their mission as the special representatives of Jesus (cf. the cognate noun "apostles" in 6:30). The notion of going out "two by two" is thoroughly Jewish (cf. Luke 10:1; Acts 8:14; 13:2; 15:40), and the "authority" on which the disciples act is derived directly from Jesus (v. 7c).

Jesus commands the disciples to take along what is essential ("staff," "tunic," "sandals"; vv. 8a, 9) but nothing more (not "bread," "knapsack," "pin-money," or extra "tunic"; vv. 8–9). The point is that they are not about to become professional itinerant preachers but have before them the eschatologically urgent task of extending Jesus' ministry to Israel. Moreover, when they enter a village, they are to stay in one house only and not move about seeking more comfortable quarters (v. 10). Should a locality not welcome them or accept their message, they are to "shake off the dust that is on their [your] feet for a testimony against them" (v. 11), that is to say, they are to give the people of that place a sign of warning to the effect that they have become as the "heathen" and stand under the judgment of God (cf. Matt. 10:14–15; Acts 13:51; 18:6).

As for the missionary journey itself, Mark writes that the disciples go out and proclaim repentance, exorcise demons, and heal the sick (vv. 12–13). This description of their mission parallels exactly the mission of Jesus (cf. 1:14–15, 32–39; 3:7–12).

Applied to the church of Mark, this text reminded these Christians that they, too, have been entrusted by Jesus with a mission. Their mission, too, is an extension of his mission.

First Lesson: Amos 7:10–15. Amos, a layman from the Judean village of Tekoa (1:1; 7:14), was sent by God around 750 B.C. to the northern kingdom of Israel to denounce its errant sense of security (cf. 6:1–3, 13), its tolerance of social injustice (cf. 3:9–10; 4:1; 5:7, 10–15), its immorality (cf. 4:1; 6:1, 4–6, 12), and its false piety (cf. 4:4–6; 5:5–6). It was towards the close of the long and prosperous reign of Jeroboam II (786–746 B.C.) that Amos undertook his ministry. He appeared publicly first in Samaria, the capital of the northern kingdom (chaps. 3–6), and then at Bethel, the site of the royal sanctuary. The setting for the text is Bethel, and it depicts Amos' clash with Amaziah, the supervising priest at the temple.

The text opens with the news that Amaziah has sent a message to King Jeroboam to the effect that Amos should be charged with treason for having conspired against the palace (v. 10). Indeed, he has so filled the land with his message of judgment that it can no longer endure another word from him (v. 10). In essence, he is predicting the violent death of the king and the deportation of the nation into exile (v. 11).

Before Jeroboam can receive the message and react, Amaziah takes it upon himself to counsel Amos. He respectfully addresses him as "seer," as a "charismatic" prophet, and advises him to return home to Judea and there prophesy for a living (v. 12). Bethel, however, is henceforth "off limits" to him, for it is a national sanctuary (v. 13).

In his reply to Amaziah, Amos punctuates his words with three references to himself ("I," v. 14) followed by three references to the "Lord" (vv. 15–16). He contends that he is neither a professional prophet (cf. 1 Sam. 9:6–10; Mic. 3:5–8, 11) nor a member of a prophetic guild (cf. 1 Kings 22:6; 2 Kings 2:3; 1 Sam. 10:5). On the contrary, he is a shepherd by profession and a dresser of sycamore trees (v. 14). The reason he prophesies as he does has nothing to do with earning a living. It is because God has interrupted his life, himself choosing him and compelling him to go and to prophesy to the people of Israel (v. 15).

Amos is the first Hebrew prophet whose words have been preserved in a book. He is also the first to proclaim the "day of the Lord" as bringing judgment upon Israel and not salvation (cf. 5:18–20; chaps. 8–9). The text admirably conveys the powerful sense of mission that one can have when one knows oneself to have been called into service by God.

Second Lesson: Eph. 1:3–14. If Paul was the author of the Letter to the Ephesians, he most likely wrote it in the early 60s while a prisoner at Rome. If he was not the author, the Epistle was most likely written in Asia Minor sometime between A.D. 80 and 100. Be that as it may, the addressees were Gentile Christians and the writer's principal topic is the church. An important facet of this topic is the oneness within the church of Jew and Gentile who, "united in Christ through his reconciling death, have access by one Spirit to the Father" (H. Chadwick, "Ephesians," *Peake's Commentary on the Bible* [London: Nelson, 1962] 980).

The text presents a variation of this thought and, in the original Greek, captures in a single sentence the fundamental contents of the letter. Formally, it is what may be termed a hymnic benediction (cf. the word "blessed" in 1:3).

By a wide margin, the single most prevalent expression in the text is "in Christ" or its equivalent ("in him," "in whom," "in the Beloved," "in the Messiah"; cf. also "through Jesus Christ"). Since the entire benediction is a paean of praise to God the Father (1:3), the repeated use of this expression shows that, for the author, the locus of God's activity towards humankind and of his revelation of himself is solely Jesus Christ.

With this in mind, we can trace the flow of the text as follows, even though the basic themes intertwine. Our praise, says the author, is to God the Father, who in Jesus Christ has poured out upon us from heaven his blessing (v. 3). In Christ, God has elected us before creation to be free from sin and resplendent before him (v. 4). In Christ, God has graciously adopted us to be his sons (vv. 5–6). In Christ, God has graciously redeemed us, granting us the forgiveness of our trespasses (vv. 7–8). And in Christ, God has revealed his will and purpose to us, namely, that in the fulness of time all things in heaven and on earth might be united under Christ's governance (vv. 9–10). And with respect to this governance, both "we" Jews and "you" Gentiles have the Spirit as a guarantee of the life to come (as a first installment which assures future payment).

Compared with the First Lesson and the Gospel for the day, this text has none of the particularity about it of the call of Amos and of the commissioning of the disciples. It is thoroughly cosmic in sweep as it treats of God's eternal purposes as worked out in the Son and sealed by the Spirit in baptism.

HOMILETICAL INTERPRETATION

1. Concern

The mission of the church is cosmic in its support and concrete in its demands.

2. Confirmations and Concretions

Henrik Ibsen's drama *Brand* depicts a man struggling through a tempestuous blizzard in the icy wastes of Norway. "Go back," an observer cries. "I can't," says Brand, "I am on a mission for someone great whose name is God."[1]

Everyone who has ever been called of God understands Brand's response. He is also likely to understand the call of the observer. That would certainly have been true of the twelve who were first sent out. They had nothing for their journey except a staff, no bread, no bag, no money. They wore sandals and had only one tunic. There were people who refused to hear them and they ran into many demons, not all of which they could cast out. But they could not go back—they were on a mission for someone great.

Nor can we! The mission to which the church is called is cosmic in its support. This is the great burden of the Epistle. The writer sees the fellowship of Christ flowing from the eternal mystery of God which unites

1. See Henrik Ibsen, *Brand* (London: Rupert Hart-Davis, 1960).

all things in heaven and earth. The language is poetic, admittedly sub-
lime. Yet unless the church understands its resources to be cosmic in their
sweep, it is soon likely to run out of energy.

God is the eternal source of blessing. He never fails to love. A grand
claim was once made for a commercial product: "Ice Never Fails." These
words were spread on a huge sign in a city on the Eastern seaboard before
refrigeration became widespread. With what confidence it spelled out its
message, "You can count on ice. Ice will never fail to preserve your food,
to cool your drinks."

That sign is laughably dated, yet strangely contemporary. The public
is still looking for something that will not fail. And others are forever
offering us some product to meet that need. Their names make their
boast. *Sure* a product is called, clearly advising us that if we use it we will
be not only more fragrant but more confident. For some time there has
been a line of sports products named *Everlast*. Such abiding security they
seemed to offer. It is always a little amusing to someone outside the boxing
ring to see some fighter keeling over from a knockout blow with the word
Everlast emblazoned on his trunks.

What a search for support we carry out! And again and again we discover in spite of all our billboards, ice *does* fail. We can not always be
sure. The things we call everlasting seem forever to be knocked out by
the temporary. Everything that is except God, who isn't a "thing" at all
but the eternal source of love who chose us in Christ even before the
foundations of the world were set in place. He is everlasting! You can be
sure of him. *God* never fails.

God never fails to care for us. The eternity of God is best expressed not
in some kind of advertising slogan but through biblical faith in which we
see his constancy revealed. God has a constant care for us and an abiding
concern for his Creation.

We have been thrilled to see the success of the Apollo-Soyuz space
experiment. We are glad that we have come to a time when Americans
and Russians can work together for mutual benefit. The handshake of
friendship takes the place of handsfull of weapons. I remember a cartoon
from the earlier years of space shots. It showed a father who had taken
his little boy out under a starry sky when one of the first satellites was
visible on the horizon. As they looked intently up at the sky the boy
pointed his finger. But the father said, "No, Son, that one has been up
there all along." The father was saying that in a time when the sky seems
filled with satellites and other kinds of hardware that go up and come
down there are still stars in the sky that have been up there all along.

The Christian faith gives us an assurance like this. We see space shots go up, we see space shots come down. We see the triumphs of technology and we are faced with the horrendous questions of priorities they raise. But God's love is like a star. We reach out toward it many times even though we cannot touch it, with the knowledge that God's love has been there all along.

This image can only suggest that aspect of God's love which becomes flesh, which walks among us. For the constancy of God is best imagined not as an object in space but as a person in history. That constancy is most real in the person of Jesus Christ who is with us to suffer when we suffer, to rejoice when we rejoice.

God never fails to do justice. The mission of the church is cosmic in its support but concrete in its demands. Amos understood that, as this Old Testament lesson makes clear, and the legacy of Amos must always be inherited by every generation in the church.

The God of biblical revelation is a just God. He measures the walls we build between people with his moral plumbline. He is the God who holds his will against the wills of men and measures our achievements by his law. Amos is called to serve *this* God. Amos is not comfortable about it. The "proper" priest says, in effect, "Amos, these are sacred precincts. We don't want that message in here." But Amos can not help trying to get that message through. He, like Ibsen's Brand, cannot turn back. He is not an official prophet nor an accredited priest. He is no part of the Establishment. But he is part of God's design. So are we.

We are never comfortable with the justice of God. But no less than Amos you and I must seek to participate in that justice. To try to voice it, but even more to embody justice. Every church, every minister, every lay person—Amos was a layman!—must be constantly involved in discovering and ministering to the concerns of persons around them.[1] This means dealing with justice in the concrete even if it means standing against the King—or a President. It means confronting the forces that make for war. It means dealing with criminal law, and with criminals in prison (with persons as well as with principles). It means coming to grips with exiles and refugees. It means plunging into the world of history.

The justice of God demands that we do all that we can to see that every person gets what is due them. There is always room for work and

---

1. One way of getting at these from a theological base may be found in *Faith Alive!: A Study Book for Doing Theology*, edited by David James Randolph (Nashville: Tidings, 1969). Compare Wallace E. Fisher, *From Tradition to Mission* (Nashville and New York: Abingdon Press, 1965) and Robert K. Hudnut, *Arousing the Sleeping Giant* (New York, Evanston, etc.: Harper and Row, 1973).

never room for self-righteousness. For the justice of God will be done, if not through us then upon us. We who would be prophets stand under that justice no less than anyone else.

The Christian mission to which you and I are called is cosmic in its support and concrete in its demands. Our love falters. Our justice is often fragmentary. Ice melts and all our sureties are at last unsure. But God never fails to care for us. God never fails to do justice. We can count on God. Trust him. Seek to walk in his way and you step on foundations laid before the world began. *Become obedient to this way, purpose in the world & your life will have meaning. You will be part of the greatest movement on earth – God's plan*

3. CONSTRUCTION

These passages suggest a sermon on the church which deals with: *to bring heaven & earth together ... to bring humanity into peace & love as we live on God's earth.*

1. Mission (the Gospel).
2. Cosmic support (the Epistle).
3. Concrete demands (OT lesson).

The Ninth Sunday after Pentecost   *7/18*

Lutheran	Roman Catholic	Episcopal	Pres./UCC/Chr.	Methodist/COCU
Jer. 23:1–6	Jer. 23:1–6	Jer. 23:1–6	Jer. 23:1–6	Jer. 23:1–6
Eph. 2:13–22	Eph. 2:13–18	Eph. 2:11–18	Eph. 2:11–18	Eph. 2:13–22
Mark 6:30–34	Mark 6:30–34	Mark 6:30–34	Mark 6:30–34	Mark 6:30–44

EXEGESIS

Gospel: Mark 6:30–34. The text spans two units: 6:30–31 and 6:32–34. Vv. 30–31 form the conclusion to the pericope on the commissioning of the twelve (6:6b–13), and vv. 32–34 introduce the miracle of the feeding of the five thousand. Taken together, however, vv. 30–34 do cohere.

Mark designates the returning disciples as "the apostles" (v. 30). Although this expression is not the technical term in the Second Gospel that it is, for example, in Paul's writings, it does have recognizable content. Thus, it is applied to the twelve and refers to the fact that Jesus "sends them out" both to preach and to exorcise ·demons (3:14–15; 6:7, 12–13). For Mark, therefore, the word "apostles" describes the twelve as those who, on the authority of Jesus, function as an extension of his ministry.

The text reports that the apostles return to Jesus and tell him of all they have done and taught (v. 30), that is, of their preaching and healing activity (6:12–13). Jesus summons them to come away to a lonely place where they can rest for awhile and find relief from the hubbub around them (v. 31; cf. 3:20). Accordingly, they leave in a boat and head for a deserted spot (v. 32). But there are many who see them embarking and recognize them, the upshot being that people from all the surrounding towns run to the place towards which Jesus and the disciples are sailing (v. 33). Getting out of the boat, Jesus sees the great crowd of people, has compassion upon them, and teaches them at length, for they are as leaderless and aimless as sheep who have no shepherd (v. 34).

In consideration of the sheep-and-shepherd imagery in the OT (cf. Num. 27:17; 1 Kings 22:17; Jer. 23:1–6; Ezek. 34), the implication of the text is that Jesus is the messianic Shepherd who in love "gathers" and through his authoritative teaching "feeds" the eschatological flock of Israel (cf. Matt. 9:35–38).

First Lesson: Jer. 23:1–6. Jeremiah began his prophetic ministry in 627 B.C. when Josiah was king of Judah (640–609 B.C.). He was active through the subsequent reigns of Jehoiakim (609–598 B.C.), Jehoiachin (598–597 B.C.), and Zedekiah (597–587 B.C.), remaining in the land even after the destruction of Jerusalem (587 B.C.). But about 582 B.C., upon the assassination of Gedaliah, the newly appointed governor of Judah, a band of Israelites, fearing reprisals from the Babylonians, fled to Egypt, taking Jeremiah with them. What became of Jeremiah in Egypt is not known.

The Book of Jeremiah falls into four main sections. The first (1:1–25:14) contains his prophecies of doom against Jerusalem and Judah, and the second (25:15–38; chaps. 46–51) his oracles against the nations. By contrast, the third section (chaps. 26–36) is devoted to his prophecies of salvation for Israel and Judah, and the final one (chaps. 37–45) is the so-called passion story of Jeremiah.

The text is located in the first main section. It comprises sayings of the Lord which have the form of threat (vv. 1–2) and promise (vv. 3–6). God's wrath, says Jeremiah, is against the shepherds, or rulers of Judah, who destroy, scatter, drive away, and neglect the flock of Israel (vv. 1–2). In their place, God himself will gather the remnant of the flock from all the countries of the world, and he will set shepherds over the sheep who will truly care for them (vv. 3–4). In point of fact, in the future God will raise up from the line of David one who will rule in accordance with his will ("a righteous Branch"), one who will be his instrument of salvation ("justice and righteousness") towards his people (v. 5). Under the governance of this ruler, Judah and Israel will be restored as one nation, so that unlike king Zedekiah, who is indebted for his throne to Nebuchadnezzar and is a mockery to his name ("the Lord is my righteousness"), this new son of David will act in full concert with his name ("the Lord is our righteousness [salvation]") (v. 6).

The text is well suited to the Gospel for the day because, for Christians, Jesus is the one in the line of David who is the true Shepherd of God's people.

Second Lesson: Eph. 2:13–22. It is said that the entire Epistle reaches its culmination in vv. 11–22. The text itself may be divided as follows: v. 13 introduces the hymn of vv. 14–18, which extols the peace Christ has established between Jew and Gentile and between God and mankind, and vv. 19–22 set forth the consequences of this peace.

The reference to the "far" and the "near" in v. 13 alludes to Isa. 57:19. But there the contrast is between Israelites in exile and Israelites in Palestine. Here the contrast is between Gentile and Jew. The thrust of v. 13 is that through the blood of Christ the Gentiles have become part of the people of God.

Intoning the great hymn of peace (vv. 14–18), the author writes that, in the person of Christ, oneness now reigns between Jew and Gentile; former hostility has given way to peace (v. 14). Through the death of Christ, the law, which served to separate Jew from Gentile, has been abolished, so that in place of these two men Christ has created one new man, the church (v. 15). What is more, in the church these two have also been reconciled by Christ to God, so that hostility between God and mankind has also been brought to an end (v. 16).

But Christ is not simply the ground and source of peace. He it is (and his ambassadors) who has likewise come and proclaimed the fact of this peace to both Jew and Gentile. Moreover, like a high priest he furthermore gives access to Jew and Gentile in the one Spirit to God the Father (v. 18).

The effective result of the peace Christ has established is that Gentiles are no more to be regarded as aliens or resident aliens as far as the household of God is concerned; in Christ they are members of this household with full citizenship-rights (v. 19). Then, too, the whole structure, with Christ as the cornerstone (cf. Isa. 28:16; Matt. 21:42), tends upwards towards God and is his dwelling place (vv. 20–22).

If the Gospel and the First Lesson emphasize the truth that Jesus is the prophesied Shepherd of the eschatological flock of Israel, this text emphasizes the truth that in Christ Gentiles, too, have their place in this flock, which is in fact the church.

HOMILETICAL INTERPRETATION

1. CONCERN

Jesus is the shepherd of his flock, the church in which Jews and Gentiles are welcome.

2. CONFIRMATIONS AND CONCRETIONS

In the Candid Camera series on television some boys were once chosen to receive what they were told was a big prize. They were paraded before their classmates and the master of ceremonies went through an elaborate buildup about their selection for the award. At the climax came the words: "You have been chosen . . . shepherds of the month!"

The looks of disappointment on the boys' faces filled the screen. Being a shepherd of the month is not very exciting to the contemporary imagination. However, if we think of the shepherd as the person who cares for a bunch of noisy, straggling creatures, then we realize how essential that task is. John Updike has a story called "Lifeguard" in which he describes the attentions which the man on the beach gives to those struggling in the waters. That image of the lifeguard may be more appropriate for our time. Try reading Psalm Twenty-three with that image in mind, "The Lord is my lifeguard."

Whether "shepherd" or some other image may be sought for the one who cares, the image of the strangers drawn from Ephesians is very real to us. Vance Packard has written a study of contemporary America entitled *A Nation of Strangers*.[1] The Christian community offers an alternative. We can be members of a community where we are strangers no more. That community is what the Letter to the Ephesians is about.

The Christian community, however, is not only a group which is concerned about internal relations. The Christian community moves out into the world to bring together all persons in a new understanding of humanity. Jesus Christ has broken down the walls between persons.

The church is potentially God's family. Several expressions of this truth are worth exploring. One is that the church should build family relationships at a time when many forces are working against this. Secondly, the church should develop family-like groups where persons may come together face to face to be truly human with one another. Thirdly,

1. Vance Packard, *A Nation of Strangers* (New York: David McKay, 1972).
See also Morton Thompson, *Not As A Stranger* (New York: Scribners, 1955).

the church can actually become the "family" for many persons, especially in our modern cities, who otherwise would live alone.

The eschatological dimension of these passages is inescapable. The privileges and demands of life in the kingdom now are enormous. At the same time we look beyond the limits of all that we know to that Jesus who transcends all our languages and our images in his eternal caring.

3. CONSTRUCTION
The concern of this sermon could be developed in the following steps:
1. The need for belonging (the OT lesson).
2. The Caring Christ (the Gospel).
3. The Church as God's family (Second Lesson).

Last Things: A Summing Up

A Theology in Outline: these lessons have offered us no less. We began with the God who addresses the valley full of bones to bring life and who calls the church into being on Pentecost. We saw how this God reveals himself as Father, Son and Holy Spirit in the lessons for Trinity Sunday. Successive lessons have provided the basis for an elemental if unsystematic study of the church in its mission to the world. The interpreter makes no claim that in this limited space all the terrain has been explored. He simply observes that it has come into view and that it is beautiful.

Faith in every specific expression reaches toward wholeness. Christian theology after all is not an arrangement of words, a collection of texts, an arbitrary categorization of data. Theology is rather a way of seeing faith in its wholeness and living life in its fullness.

Thus the preacher who understands his task knows himself not to be serving snacks from his own little kitchen but breaking the Bread of Life to the hungry. This truth will shame him, for he knows how often he has handed out crumbs. But it will also redeem him, for is not he who breaks the Bread also nourished by it?

In any case, it is appropriate that these lessons end on eschatological themes, even as doctrine dealing with the Holy Spirit has from ancient times.

"Last Things" is the language often associated with eschatology and the title of a novel by C. P. Snow. In it we read a kind of summary of a series of books dealing with a scholar who comes to walk "the corridors of power" in Great Britain. In the novel, the central character tells his son that he has refused a job in the government. The son observes that this must be the end of one line for him. The father agrees. The son asks, "It never was a very central line, though, was it?"[1]

Soon or late we all come to the end of one line, the line of our earthly life. Christian faith does not alter that. Christian faith simply guarantees that the life lived in loving God, neighbor, and self is the central line. You can know that you have not been sidetracked in selfishness.

The central line of God's purpose is a great line to be on. I heard once of a minor employee in a small British rail station who was meticulously going about his work. A skeptical tourist asked why he was doing such a thorough job in such an obscure place, visited by so few people. In amazement the workman replied that though his was a small station it was part of the national system! He felt involved in a mighty transportation network. Those who do Christian work may feel that their labors are insignificant, their work unrecognized. But these lessons remind us that however remote from the heavenly our daily tasks may seem, Christian discipleship carries us on the central line.

The central line has a destiny beyond all earthly destinations. The Christian "looks to the resurrection and the life of the world to come."

F. Scott Fitzgerald knew and described the wasteland of modernity as few have. At the conclusion of his novel, *The Great Gatsby*, the narrator Nick Carraway wanders down to the beach at Gatsby's house and sits brooding. He thinks back to the time Gatsby looked across the waters of Long Island Sound and first saw the green light at the end of Daisy Buchanan's dock.

"Gatsby believed in the green light, the orgiastic future that year by year recedes before us. It eluded us then, but that's no matter. Tomorrow we will run faster, stretch our arms farther. . . . And one fine morning——

"So we beat our boats against the current, borne back ceaselessly into the past."[2]

It is often claimed that Gatsby represents the "great American dream." If so, no wonder there is a wasteland. Gatsby confuses quantity with quality. He seems to know the surface of everything and the depth of nothing. Fitzgerald, moralist as well as storyteller, knew that. But had Fitzgerald been writing of the Christian hope instead of the American dream he would have written a different story. The story would have been set in the Wasteland but it would be about a person who finds the Christ leading him to the living water. It would picture a life refreshed by the

---

1. C. P. Snow, *Last Things* (New York: Scribners, 1970), p. 137.
2. F. Scott Fitzgerald, *The Great Gatsby* in *Three Novels* (New York: Scribners, 1953), p. 137.

waters of grace, waters which irrigate the wasteland with the possibility of renewal. That story might conclude:

The Christian believes in the green light, the joyful future that day by day comes toward us. We never completely grasp it in any one day, but that's no problem, because tomorrow we will respond more fully, stretch out our arms farther. . . . And one bright morning——

So we sail on, boats with the current, borne ceaselessly toward God.